Love
Is an
Action Verb

Couples Therapy
Workbook

LAURA SILVERSTEIN

*This Couples
Therapy Workbook
belongs to:*

Partner 1

_____

Partner 2

_____

Book design by Adam Hay Studio

ISBN: 979-8-9854643-3-7

CONTENTS

Glossary of Worksheets and Exercises

"To be deeply loved by someone gives you strength, but to love someone deeply gives you courage." [1]

Often attributed to Lao Tzu

Introduction
Is This Workbook For You?

Being a relationship counselor is easier than you might think. It's kind of like hosting a potluck for two. I set the table, provide the utensils, and send out an invitation for the time and place. Then the couple shows up to do all the hard work. This process can be life-changing and extraordinarily effective at helping people feel more loved. I have had the opportunity to watch couples fall back in love, learn how to be kinder to each other, and sometimes help them navigate a peaceful, respectful separation.

Most of what I do is ask guided questions and keep conversations on track. When couples arrive in my office with curiosity, a willingness to work hard, and just enough humility, they make excellent progress. A book cannot replace couples therapy with a licensed provider. I call this a "Couples Therapy Workbook" because I have extracted the aspects of couples therapy that can be done on your own. Think of these exercises as homework you might do between sessions to practice skills and deepen understanding.

But it won't be easy. A workbook requires you to put pen to paper and apply the skills right here, right now. As you work through the pages of this resource, I'll be coaching you to talk to each other in a specific way about important elements of your relationship. You'll have these conversations by answering self-reflective questions, interviewing each other, and following ground rules to set you up for success. Love is not a luxury; it is a core need. I want to help you two to co-create the love you deserve.

The DIY Relationship Self Help Series

This couples therapy workbook is the newest addition to the DIY Relationship Self Help Series. My first book, *Love Is an Action Verb, Stop Wasting Time and Delight in Your Relationship* is written to read on your own to learn how to show up for your partner as the best version of yourself. It is a traditional relationship self-help book based on the research of John Gottman, Sue Johnson, Daniel Goleman, and other experts in the field. It is a comprehensive resource that explains relational psychology theory and research in jargon-free language, with many real-world examples, stories, metaphors, and diagrams.

This workbook, *Love Is an Action Verb: Couples Therapy Workbook,* is designed for you and your partner to read and complete *together*, instead of alone. Some exercises are collaborative, and other exercises can be first done alone, before you share your answers.

Each of these books function as a stand-alone resource. That is to say, you can pick up either off the shelf and dive into the material without missing any crucial information. That said, you might enjoy reading these two books in tandem. As you complete the exercises in this workbook, you might want more real-life examples, or a deeper understanding of the theories and research that inform my recommendations. The chapters in both books are organized in the same order and with the same theme. So, for example, if you are working on intimacy in the workbook, it will be easy to find more background in the corresponding chapter of the first book.

What to Expect in this Workbook

There are two core elements to this couples therapy workbook: reaching your relationship goals and sustaining your connection. You are more likely to achieve your goals when you write them down, develop a plan, and make intentional changes. The best way to improve any skill is through practice and repetition. If you both believe that it "takes two to tango," and are invested in improving your relationship, then this workbook is for you. You'll start by reminding yourselves why you fell in love in the first place, then you'll learn ground rules and strategies to improve communication and intimacy, and last you'll make a maintenance plan keep your relationship strong.

> **Note:** No book can take the place of therapy with a licensed relationship expert. I have never met you, nor completed an assessment and treatment plan. This book contains suggestions and practices that work for many couples, but not all. *Please do not follow any advice that does not feel right or comfortable for any reason.*
>
> This workbook is intended to create a fun and positive experience for you both. While it requires time and effort, I don't want it to cause distress for either of you. If this starts to happen, simply put it down and continue at another time.

Why Listen to Me?

The advice I'm giving you is not coming from the top of my head. I only know what I know because I have had the extreme privilege of learning from some of the most brilliant relationship experts in the world. I have been passionate about human interaction since middle school, and have been looking for great teachers ever since. I have been lucky enough to find generous mentors on every leg of my professional journey.

I have probably been most influenced by Drs. John and Julie Gottman, who I met early in my training. In 2011, I achieved the highest level of clinical training in the Gottman Method of Couples Therapy, and I also train other therapists in this model and educate the public in media outlets such as the *New York Times*, *Cosmopolitan*, and *Real Simple Magazine*. The Gottman Method[1] is a framework for teaching therapists how to guide couples through the process of improving their relationships based on three decades of longitudinal studies, scientific research, and analysis.

My husband and I co-founded a group psychotherapy practice specializing in couples therapy and we oversee a team that provides a combined total of over 5,000 hours of counseling every year. I continue to learn how to be a better therapist every single day from each client who is brave enough to walk through our doors.

This workbook is built on the knowledge of theoreticians, clinicians, scientists, clients, and my own lived experience. Since I have trained with so many mentors, sometimes I don't know what language is my own and what is me repeating something brilliant that I heard at a workshop 15 years ago. The recommendations and strategies in this workbook are not solely my own; together they represent the integration of what I have learned along the way.

While the concepts are not 100% my own, they are an attempt to share this knowledge in a new hands-on format. Some people have the privilege to be able to access and hire a private couples therapist, but many do not. My sincere hope is that this workbook can reach people who are inspired to improve their relatinships in a different way.

Our dilemma is that we hate change and love it at the same time; what we really want is for things to remain the same but get better."[1]

Sydney Harris

How This Workbook Is Organized

Each chapter addresses a different relationship skill, explains the background and research behind the recommendations, and provides hands-on exercises to master the strategies. Every chapter ends with a Chapter Overview, summarizing the main theme of the lesson, and a Chapter Challenge, which is a short action-oriented prompt designed to be done by the end of the next day.

The exercises you'll be doing alone are identified as "independent," and the ones you'll do together are labeled, "joint." Some couples like to sit down together while completing the entire workbook, and others prefer to do the reading and independent exercises separately and then come together for the joint exercises (or a combination of both). I recommend experimenting with different approaches to see what works best for you. Try not to peek at your partner's answers before answering your own. With most exercises, you'll share your responses after you both complete them.

Throughout the book, you will encounter a fictional couple, Carson and Jamie. I created these characters to help demonstrate dialogue and illustrate what to do and what not to do.

> **Note:** I assure you, Carson and Jamie are entirely fictional. If you are a client of mine, or you know me in another context, any similarities with you or someone you know are completely coincidental.

What Is NOT Included in This Workbook

A lot of relationship self-help books are targeted toward specific religious groups, types of relationships, or traditional definitions of marriage. I will not be making any assumptions about who you are or how you love. The suggestions in this book are designed to be applicable to anyone who wants to be in a happy, meaningful relationship.

There are many aspects of relationship health that I believe are better served in a different context than a DIY workbook. For this reason, I won't be giving recommendations about how to manage trauma, early childhood dynamics, or racial, gender, and ethnic differences. If you are in a consensually non-monogamous relationship and plan to use this workbook with more than two people, I recommend working in pairs first and then creatively finding a way to integrate the exercises into your specific situation.

With that in mind, this workbook might **not** be right for you at this time. Take the short quiz on the next page as a self-reflection tool to decided whether or not this workbook is what you need right now.

Here is your first exercise!
Pre-Workbook Questionnaire
*Independent Exercise: **Partner One***

Instructions

Answer the following questions to determine whether or not you feel this workbook is right for you at this time.

1. Are you currently in a primary romantic relationship? ☐ Yes ☐ No ☐ Unsure

2. Overall, do you love and respect your partner and feel loved and respected (aside from fleeting feelings after a fight)? ☐ Yes ☐ No ☐ Unsure

3. Are you certain that you want to stay in this relationship? ☐ Yes ☐ No ☐ Unsure

4. Do you have time and energy right now to devote to self-improvement and personal development? ☐ Yes ☐ No ☐ Unsure

5. Are you open to looking at your own contributions (both positive and negative) to your relationship happiness? ☐ Yes ☐ No ☐ Unsure

6. Based on your answers to these questions, do you feel this workbook is a good fit for what you are looking for right now? ☐ Yes ☐ No ☐ Unsure

> If you answered **No** or **Unsure** to any of the questions above, some of the recommendations may not apply to your situation. I recommend that you modify the exercises accordingly.

7. Why did you pick up this workbook? (Put a check mark next to all that apply)

☐ I enjoyed reading 'Love Is an Action Verb' and want to apply what I learned together with my partner.

☐ We are in the beginning stages of a new relationship and want to learn what experts recommend so that we can start off right.

☐ I believe our relationship is in good shape and I want to keep learning and growing so that it stays strong.

☐ Life has been busy and our relationship has moved to the back burner. I picked up this workbook to get back on track.

☐ Our relationship is in crisis. We are working through it, and want a resource to help us focus on positivity and review foundational recommendations.

Here is your first exercise!

Pre-Workbook Questionnaire
Independent Exercise: Partner Two

Instructions

Answer the following questions to determine whether or not you feel this workbook is right for you at this time.

1. Are you currently in a primary romantic relationship? ☐ Yes ☐ No ☐ Unsure

2. Overall, do you love and respect your partner and feel loved and respected (aside from fleeting feelings after a fight)? ☐ Yes ☐ No ☐ Unsure

3. Are you certain that you want to stay in this relationship? ☐ Yes ☐ No ☐ Unsure

4. Do you have time and energy right now to devote to self-improvement and personal development? ☐ Yes ☐ No ☐ Unsure

5. Are you open to looking at your own contributions (both positive and negative) to your relationship happiness? ☐ Yes ☐ No ☐ Unsure

6. Based on your answers to these questions, do you feel this workbook is a good fit for what you are looking for right now? ☐ Yes ☐ No ☐ Unsure

> If you answered **No** or **Unsure** to any of the questions above, some of the recommendations may not apply to your situation. I recommend that you modify the exercises accordingly.

7. Why did you pick up this workbook? (Put a check mark next to all that apply)

☐ I enjoyed reading 'Love Is an Action Verb' and want to apply what I learned together with my partner.

☐ We are in the beginning stages of a new relationship and want to learn what experts recommend so that we can start off right.

☐ I believe our relationship is in good shape and I want to keep learning and growing so that it stays strong.

☐ Life has been busy and our relationship has moved to the back burner. I picked up this workbook to get back on track.

☐ Our relationship is in crisis. We are working through it, and want a resource to help us focus on positivity and review foundational recommendations.

If you are experiencing any of these symptoms, this workbook is not indicated, and you may be at risk:

Fear of your partner

Emotional manipulation

Physical or psychological abuse

Call 988 or 1-800-273-8255 (US)

Or seek the support of a licensed professional.

A Word of Caution

There are infinite ways to hurt someone when you are angry or feeling attacked. In martial arts movies, you'll see a master can use any inanimate object as a deadly killing tool – even a ballpoint pen!

Though these exercises are intended to encourage vulnerability toward the goal of feeling closer, I caution you that **vulnerability can be weaponized**. For example, your partner might share something painful, or take accountability for a mistake they made. If you throw this back at them later, during a fight, or when making a point, your partner might regret being vulnerable. This could cause them to shut down and be less open, or they could counter-attack with something from these workbook exercises that you admitted. If this happens, it discourages both parties from continuing to be vulnerable and honest with each other and you won't get the full benefit of these exercises. Therefore, please make a commitment to yourself and your partner not to weaponize any part of this workbook.

Thank You for Being Here!

Congratulations to you both for picking up this workbook. It is a significant accomplishment to commit to carving out time to nurture yourself, your partner, and your relationship. It is my sincere hope that the exercises in this workbook will lead you to feel happier, more connected, and deeply loved.

There are many factors that contribute to who you are as a couple and as individuals. If any of my language or examples do not resonate with you, please either translate the advice according to your specific circumstances or move on to a different section of the book.

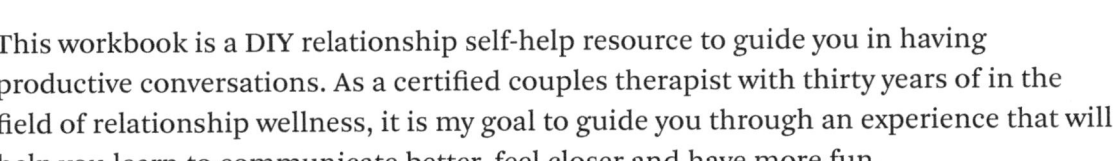

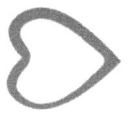 # Chapter Takeaway

This workbook is a DIY relationship self-help resource to guide you in having productive conversations. As a certified couples therapist with thirty years of in the field of relationship wellness, it is my goal to guide you through an experience that will help you learn to communicate better, feel closer and have more fun.

 # Chapter Challenge

Your first Chapter Challenge is to turn to your partner *right now* and thank them for completing this workbook with you.

Read on to Chapter 1 where you will set your relationship goals and make a plan so that you can reach them.

"If you have built castles in the air, your work need not be lost; that is where they should be. Now put the foundations under them."[1]

Henry David Thoreau

Chapter 1
How to Set Your Relationship Goals
So that you can achieve them

*The word "love" is both a noun and a verb. As a **noun**, one might say, "I am looking for love" or "I've found love." As a **verb** one might say "I love you." And if we take an even deeper dive, love is an **action** verb. Action verbs are distinct from other kinds of verbs insofar as they reflect what someone or something can **do** (example: I jump), rather than a state of being (example: I **have** a headache).*

This short grammar reminder can dramatically influence how one approaches relationship wellness. Advice that focuses on love as a noun or a passive verb is limiting. If love were an inanimate object, it would not grow or change. The truth is relationships are living systems, and couples can work to make improvements to feel closer and happier.

Nowhere in this workbook will I suggest that you change who you are at your core. The strategies involve building skills and making slight behavioral improvements.

Are Relationships Hard Work?

The short answer is "sometimes." People who work hard and have high expectations tend to be happier than those who don't. Some parts of working on your relationship are fun and easy, and other parts are a bit harder. As with most things, the clearer you are about your goals and the more effort you put in, the greater your results will be.

The exercises in this chapter are focused on clarifying your goals and developing an action plan. Complete the next exercise, "What Are Your Goals" to clarify your hopes and expectations for completing this workbook.

What Are Your Relationship Goals?
Independent Exercise: Partner One

Instructions *Check off the statements that resonate, then go back and put a star next to your top three goals.*

☐ I want to learn how to be the best partner I can be. (Chapters 1–12)

☐ I want to feel more loved and appreciated. (Chapters 2, 6, 8–12)

☐ I want to do a better job of making sure my partner feels loved and appreciated. (Chapters 2, 6, 8–12)

☐ I want our conversations to feel more productive. (Chapters 3–7)

☐ I want a list of communication ground rules to follow. (Chapter 3)

☐ I want to fight less. (Chapters 2–7)

☐ I want to feel more understood. (Chapters 8, 9)

☐ I want to learn how to empathize better. (Chapters 8, 9)

☐ I want to build intimacy. (Chapters 10, 11)

☐ I want to build trust. (Chapters 8–10)

☐ I want to feel closer to my partner. (Chapters 8–12)

☐ I want to feel more known. (Chapters 6, 8–12)

☐ I want to have more fun together. (Chapter 11)

☐ I want to set up healthy daily relationship routines. (Chapter 10)

☐ I want to feel inspired to reach our hopes and dreams together. (Chapters 10–12)

☐ I want to manage stress better with my partner. (Chapter 8)

☐ I want our love to last a life-time. (Chapter 11)

What Are Your Relationship Goals?
Independent Exercise: *Partner Two*

Instructions *Check off the statements that resonate, then go back and put a star next to your top three goals.*

☐ I want to learn how to be the best partner I can be. (Chapters 1–12)

☐ I want to feel more loved and appreciated. (Chapters 2, 6, 8–12)

☐ I want to do a better job of making sure my partner feels loved and appreciated. (Chapters 2, 6, 8–12)

☐ I want our conversations to feel more productive. (Chapters 3–7)

☐ I want a list of communication ground rules to follow. (Chapter 3)

☐ I want to fight less. (Chapters 2–7)

☐ I want to feel more understood. (Chapters 8, 9)

☐ I want to learn how to empathize better. (Chapters 8, 9)

☐ I want to build intimacy. (Chapters 10, 11)

☐ I want to build trust. (Chapters 8–10)

☐ I want to feel closer to my partner. (Chapters 8–12)

☐ I want to feel more known. (Chapters 6, 8–12)

☐ I want to have more fun together. (Chapter 11)

☐ I want to set up healthy daily relationship routines. (Chapter 10)

☐ I want to feel inspired to reach our hopes and dreams together. (Chapters 10–12)

☐ I want to manage stress better with my partner. (Chapter 8)

☐ I want our love to last a life-time. (Chapter 11)

Make Your Plan
Joint Exercise

Now that you've identified your relationship goals, use the planning tool below to decide how you are going to use this workbook to help you reach them.
There are two options for how to proceed.

1. You can work through all the chapters in order. (Ideal for couples looking for help with one or two specific topics.)

2. You can choose where to start based on the goals you identified in the "What Are Your Goals" exercise above . (Ideal for couples looking for help with one

Instructions *Identify your top three goals by taking turns asking each other the questions below.*

1. What did you choose as your top three goals?

2. What goals do we have in common?

3. What items on the list stand out as strengths we already have?

4. Do you have a preference about whether we work through this workbook in order, or skip to a specific chapter? (If so, which chapter would you like to start with?)

5. Would you prefer to approach this workbook all at once, like a weekend workshop, or complete it chapter by chapter spread over the next few weeks?

Solidify your plan. Discuss which days, times, and locations you think will work best, and fill in the blanks below when you decide.

Day
....

Times
....

Locations
....

Congratulations on your commitment to relationship happiness!

Here is a summary of the topics that will be addressed in each remaining chapter:

- **Chapter 2:** Increasing positivity
- **Chapter 3:** Communication ground rules
- **Chapter 4:** Understanding your conflict styles
- **Chapter 5:** Asking for what you need
- **Chapter 6:** Responding to criticism
- **Chapter 7:** Taking a time-out when conversations escalate
- **Chapter 8:** Feeling more understood and dealing with stress
- **Chapter 9:** Increasing the three types of intimacy
- **Chapter 10:** Building a relationship routine to keep love alive
- **Chapter 11:** Having more fun

Each chapter will take an average of 45–90 minutes to complete in its entirety and each exercise will take about 10–15 minutes.

 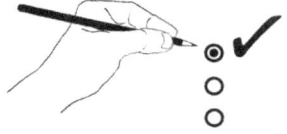

Chapter Takeaway

Love is an action verb. Since the grass is greener where you water it, it will take deliberate work to reach your relationship goals. You are more likely to achieve fulfillment when you take the time to set your goals, map out a plan, and commit to following it.

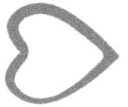 

Chapter Challenge

Take a picture of your plan from the previous exercise and schedule your work sessions in your calendar(s).

In the next chapter you'll learn what leads to long-term relationship happiness.

*"Love is blind, and
lovers cannot see,
The pretty follies that
themselves commit."*[1]

William Shakespeare

Chapter 2
How to Actually Be Happy
The life-changing power of positivity

Is love blind? Shakespeare was the first person to use this metaphor in the Merchant of Venice. Usually the term, "love is blind" is used to reference times when couples are so happy that they don't notice annoyances or faults in their partner. But love can also be blind in the other direction: sometimes positive traits and strengths become invisible when couples are only focused on their problems.

True love is, in fact, far from blind. Loving someone deeply includes seeing them for who they are, warts and all. Over time you will learn things about your partner that you don't like. There will be things that get on your nerves, and they'll let you down sometimes. Relationship satisfaction is achieved when couples notice both positive **and** negative qualities.[2] Happiness is not a process of ignoring negativity; it comes from accepting imperfection and actively reminding yourself why and how you fell in love in the first place.

Take the "Love Is Blind Quiz" on the next page to reflect on the current presence of positivity in your relationship.

Love Is Blind – True or False Quiz
Independent Exercise: Partner One

Instructions *Answer the following true or false questions. This exercise is for self-reflection purposes only. There are no right or wrong answers.*

1. My partner has both amazing and annoying qualities.

   Very True ○ ○ ○ ○ ○ Very False
           1 2 3 4 5

2. I have both amazing and annoying qualities.

   Very True ○ ○ ○ ○ ○ Very False
           1 2 3 4 5

3. Sometimes I find myself focusing more on my partner's negative qualities than their positive ones.

   Very True ○ ○ ○ ○ ○ Very False
           1 2 3 4 5

4. Sometimes I find myself focusing more on my negative qualities than the positive ones.

   Very True ○ ○ ○ ○ ○ Very False
           1 2 3 4 5

5. I can be overly self-critical.

   Very True ○ ○ ○ ○ ○ Very False
           1 2 3 4 5

6. I can be overly critical of my partner.

   Very True ○ ○ ○ ○ ○ Very False
           1 2 3 4 5

7. I think I'd be happier day to day if I were focusing more on the positive qualities in our relationship than the negative ones.

   Very True ○ ○ ○ ○ ○ Very False
           1 2 3 4 5

8. Sometimes I worry that if I try too hard to be positive, I'll come across as phony or fake.

   Very True ○ ○ ○ ○ ○ Very False
           1 2 3 4 5

9. It doesn't feel good when I get into a negative headspace, and only think about the problems in our relationship.

   Very True ○ ○ ○ ○ ○ Very False
           1 2 3 4 5

10. I'd like to focus more on the positive aspects of myself, my partner and my relationship.

    Very True ○ ○ ○ ○ ○ Very False
            1 2 3 4 5

Share your responses and insights with your partner after each of you has completed your quiz.

Love Is Blind – True or False Quiz
Independent Exercise: *Partner Two*

Instructions — *Answer the following true or false questions. This exercise is for self-reflection purposes only. There are no right or wrong answers.*

1. My partner has both amazing and annoying qualities.

   Very True   ○   ○   ○   ○   ○   Very False
             1   2   3   4   5

2. I have both amazing and annoying qualities.

   Very True   ○   ○   ○   ○   ○   Very False
             1   2   3   4   5

3. Sometimes I find myself focusing more on my partner's negative qualities than their positive ones.

   Very True   ○   ○   ○   ○   ○   Very False
             1   2   3   4   5

4. Sometimes I find myself focusing more on my negative qualities than the positive ones.

   Very True   ○   ○   ○   ○   ○   Very False
             1   2   3   4   5

5. I can be overly self-critical.

   Very True   ○   ○   ○   ○   ○   Very False
             1   2   3   4   5

6. I can be overly critical of my partner.

   Very True   ○   ○   ○   ○   ○   Very False
             1   2   3   4   5

7. I think I'd be happier day to day if I were focusing more on the positive qualities in our relationship than the negative ones.

   Very True   ○   ○   ○   ○   ○   Very False
             1   2   3   4   5

8. Sometimes I worry that if I try too hard to be positive, I'll come across as phony or fake.

   Very True   ○   ○   ○   ○   ○   Very False
             1   2   3   4   5

9. It doesn't feel good when I get into a negative headspace, and only think about the problems in our relationship.

   Very True   ○   ○   ○   ○   ○   Very False
             1   2   3   4   5

10. I'd like to focus more on the positive aspects of myself, my partner and my relationship.

   Very True   ○   ○   ○   ○   ○   Very False
             1   2   3   4   5

♡ Share your responses and insights with your partner after each of you has completed your quiz.

The Power of Positivity

Positivity is good for your health, your relationship, and overall happiness. Focusing on strengths instead of challenges in yourself, your partner and your relationship can lead to a more pleasant day to day life and it is often easier to tend to problem areas when you are operating from a foundation of appreciation and gratitude.

Dr. John Gottman and Dr. Robert Levenson published a research study that led to the ability to predict divorce with 90% accuracy.[2] Their research indicates that positivity was one of the core predictors of relationship satisfaction, stability, and longevity. The research showed that couples in healthy relationships had twenty positive interactions for every one negative interaction, compared to ailing couples who displayed an equal number of positive and negative interactions and a 5:1 ratio during times of conflict. Positive interactions were coded by behaviors such as a smile, a squeeze of the hand, or a spontaneous compliment.

Although happier relationships display more positivity, it won't work to just try to be nicer or force optimism. You can't just **say** something positive, you have to **believe** it. When a relationship is in a negative state, couples can turn things around by making internal mindset changes so that their words and actions are genuine and sincere.

If you are looking for problems, you will find them. If you are looking for beauty, you will find that as well.

The remainder of this chapter will guide you through focusing on the positive aspects of your partner so that you can bring more authentic generosity and gratitude into your interactions. In later chapters, I will provide you with communication and conflict management skills to deal with the difficulties in your relationship. We are not brushing problems under a rug; we are simply focusing on the strengths **in addition to** the problem spots.

The next series of exercises are designed to help you consciously direct your energy toward what you love about your partner. You might notice some negativity creeping in, which is normal. If this happens, try to ignore the internal critic and re-focus your energy.

"People only see what they are prepared to see." [3]

Ralph Waldo Emerson

Your Partner's Strengths Checklist
Independent Exercise: *Partner One*

Instructions *Check all the qualities below that your partner possesses.*

☐ Adventurous	☐ Affectionate	☐ Ambitious
☐ Analytical	☐ Artistic	☐ Athletic
☐ Attractive	☐ Authentic	☐ Beautiful
☐ Chill	☐ Clever	☐ Creative
☐ Curious	☐ Enthusiastic	☐ Fashionable
☐ Fearless	☐ Flexible	☐ Friendly
☐ Fun	☐ Funny	☐ Generous
☐ Good at tech	☐ Good cook	☐ Good with money
☐ Great listener	☐ Great problem-solver	☐ Great team-player
☐ Grounded	☐ Handy	☐ Hard-working
☐ Honest	☐ Humble	☐ Independent
☐ Kind	☐ Loving	☐ Loyal
☐ Nice smile	☐ Open-minded	☐ Optimistic
☐ Passionate	☐ Patient	☐ Reliable
☐ Resilient	☐ Romantic	☐ Smart
☐ Strong	☐ Sexy	☐ Thoughtful
☐ Vulnerable	☐ Warm	☐ Wise

Share your responses with your partner and give an example of a time you noticed the quality shine.

Your Partner's Strengths Checklist
Independent Exercise: *Partner Two*

Instructions   *Check all the qualities below that your partner possesses.*

☐ Adventurous   ☐ Affectionate   ☐ Ambitious

☐ Analytical   ☐ Artistic   ☐ Athletic

☐ Attractive   ☐ Authentic   ☐ Beautiful

☐ Chill   ☐ Clever   ☐ Creative

☐ Curious   ☐ Enthusiastic   ☐ Fashionable

☐ Fearless   ☐ Flexible   ☐ Friendly

☐ Fun   ☐ Funny   ☐ Generous

☐ Good at tech   ☐ Good cook   ☐ Good with money

☐ Great listener   ☐ Great problem-solver   ☐ Great team-player

☐ Grounded   ☐ Handy   ☐ Hard-working

☐ Honest   ☐ Humble   ☐ Independent

☐ Kind   ☐ Loving   ☐ Loyal

☐ Nice smile   ☐ Open-minded   ☐ Optimistic

☐ Passionate   ☐ Patient   ☐ Reliable

☐ Resilient   ☐ Romantic   ☐ Smart

☐ Strong   ☐ Sexy   ☐ Thoughtful

☐ Vulnerable   ☐ Warm   ☐ Wise

Share your responses with your partner and give an example of a time you noticed the quality shine.

Fill-In-The-Blank Love Letter
Independent Exercise: **Partner One**

Instructions ▸ Practice authentic positivity by writing a love letter to your partner. You may use the prompts below or you may prefer to write your love letter on a piece of stationery or a beautiful note card. Cross out any prompts that don't resonate and replace them with your own words.

Date:
....

Dear

I love and appreciate you very much. Maybe I don't tell you enough that

....

I think the first moment I knew I was in love with you was

....

One of the fondest memories I have of our relationship is when

....

I am looking forward to doing so many things with you, such as

....

We have so much fun together when we

....

There are so many things that I have learned from you. You have taught me

....

When our relationship is at its best, I feel like I can

....

Thank you for

....

I love you!

....

Love,

....

Share your love letter with your partner after each of you has completed writing.

Fill-In-The-Blank Love Letter
Independent Exercise: **Partner Two**

Instructions *Practice authentic positivity by writing a love letter to your partner. You may use the prompts below or you may prefer to write your love letter on a piece of stationery or a beautiful note card. Cross out any prompts that don't resonate and replace them with your own words.*

Date:
....

Dear

I love and appreciate you very much. Maybe I don't tell you enough that

....

I think the first moment I knew I was in love with you was

....

One of the fondest memories I have of our relationship is when

....

I am looking forward to doing so many things with you, such as

....

We have so much fun together when we

....

There are so many things that I have learned from you. You have taught me

....

When our relationship is at its best, I feel like I can

....

Thank you for
....

I love you!
....

Love,
....

Share your love letter with your partner after each of you has completed writing.

"Happiness is not something ready-made. It comes from your own actions"[4]

Dalai Lama XIV (Tenzin Gyatso)

 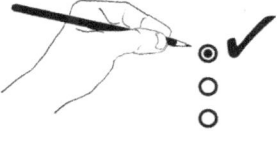

Chapter Takeaway

Love, it seems, is far from blind. Authentic happiness results from consciously looking to see the positivity around you without ignoring real problems. Focusing on the things you treasure about yourselves and your relationship will allow a foundation of appreciation that will likely help you feel more inspired to do the difficult work that relationships require.

Chapter Challenge

Catch your partner doing something good! By the end of the day tomorrow, find an opportunity to say thank you, or express fondness to your partner when they least expect it.

The next few chapters will address communication and conflict management strategies.

"It's important to make sure that we're talking with each other in a way that heals, not in a way that wounds."[1]

Barack Obama

Chapter 3
How to Avoid a Fight
Laura's 5 Communication Ground Rules to follow in every conversation

This chapter is about how to avoid "dumb," unnecessary, time-consuming arguments. You can save a lot of time avoiding this type of fight by learning and following ground rules in your dialogues. Instead of spending hours cleaning up hurt feelings and misunderstandings on the back end, these guidelines may help you prevent them altogether.

What Makes a Good Communicator?

Good communicators enjoy the benefits of mutual understanding, collaborative decision-making, and quick problem-solving. You are probably surrounded by both good communicators and poor communicators, but you might not be able to put your finger on what they are doing differently. There are subtle ways to smooth out dialogues and create a culture for interesting and engaging conversations, and there are easy traps to fall into that create miscommunication and arguments.

This chapter will provide insight into how verbal communication can succeed or fail. Some people grew up with role models who emulated compromise and conflict management strategies, and other people learned bad habits they are now trying to unlearn. As an adult, you can now choose the role models who have a communication style that you admire.

Who Are the Good Communicators in Your Life?
Independent Exercise: **Partner One**

Instructions ▸ *Answer the questions below in the space provided.*

1. List three people you consider to be excellent communicators.

....

2. How do you feel when you're talking to them?

....

3. What have you observed them doing or saying that works well?

....

Who Are the Good Communicators in Your Life?
Independent Exercise: **Partner Two**

Instructions ▸ *Answer the questions below in the space provided.*

1. List three people you consider to be excellent communicators.

....

2. How do you feel when you're talking to them?

....

3. What have you observed them doing or saying that works well?

....

Share Your Answers
Joint Exercise

Instructions ▸ *Take turns sharing your responses and insights from the exercise above.*

The following pages provide you with a list of five communication ground rules to follow for every verbal interaction in your relationship. They are not foolproof, but they will help you avoid some predictable communication traps.

Here is the list of rules that will be detailed throughout this chapter:

Laura's 5 Communication Ground Rules

1. Never place the word "that" or "like" after the words "I feel."

2. Never follow words of appreciation or apology with a conjunction (such as "and" or "but").

3. Use "I" not "you" except before a compliment.

4. Avoid run-on sentences, comma splices, and sentence sprawls.

5. Never say "never," "always," or "finally."

Rule #1

Never Place the Word "That" or "Like" after the Words "I Feel"

You have probably heard that you're supposed to "talk about your feelings" to have a good relationship. It's true. Connection and trust are built through emotional vulnerability. But if you do try to talk about your feelings and it's not working, you may be making the very common error of breaking Rule #1.

When you start a sentence with the words "I feel," you are not talking about your emotions unless your next word is an emotion. If you say "like" or "that" after "I feel" you are talking about thoughts or opinions. This causes frustration because your listener doesn't hear the emotional vulnerability they are expecting (even unconsciously). To avoid this error, simply make sure that when you start a sentence with the words "I feel," your next word is an emotion.

Examples

- **Incorrect:** I feel *that* you're wrong.

- **Correct:** I feel *frustrated* by what I'm hearing.

Rule #1 Practice Worksheet
Joint Exercise

Instructions *Work together to catch the stop words by circling the words "that" or "like" in the statements below. (See the Answer Key at the back of this book to check your work.).*

1. I feel like you need a new job.

2. I feel that the best way for us to be closer is for you to stop checking your email every five seconds.

3. I feel irritated when you look at your phone while we're talking.

4. I feel like I'm the only one working on this relationship.

5. I feel lonely when you have to work late.

6. I feel overwhelmed by everything that's on my plate right now.

7. I feel like you don't like spending time with me.

8. I feel that we only have sex when I initiate.

9. I feel shy about initiating sex.

10. I feel like I'm invisible.

Talk to Your Partner about Your Feelings

Joint Exercise

Take turns asking each other how you feel and listening to your responses to the conversation prompts. Use the Feelings List on the following page for guidance.

1. How are you feeling about doing this workbook together?

2. Tell me about a time when you felt happy.

3. Tell me about a time when you felt frustrated.

4. Tell me about a time when you felt overwhelmed.

5. How are you feeling about your relationships with extended family?

6. How are you feeling about the state of our country?

7. How are you feeling about our neighborhood/community?

8. How are you feeling about our home/household?

9. Tell me what kind of things have been worrying you lately.

10. Tell me about a time you felt proud of yourself or someone you love.

Feelings Checklist

Feelings that are generally unpleasant	**Feelings that are generally pleasant**	**Feelings that are generally neither pleasant nor unpleasant**
Angry	Happy	Fine
Frustrated	Content	Indifferent
Irritated	Excited	Neutral
Sad	Satisfied	Uninterested
Left out	Curious	Unaffected
Resentful	Proud	Impartial
Worried	Confident	Content
Nervous	Hopeful	Apathetic
Anxious	Encouraged	Aware
Jealous	Grateful	
Aggravated	Pleased	
Frightened	Delighted	
Terrified	Overjoyed	
Uneasy	Compassionate	
Tense	Inspired	
Overwhelmed	Amused	
Hopeless	Joyful	
Helpless	Calm	
Disappointed	Peaceful	
Lonely	Loving	
Alienated	Admiration	
Dismissed	Interested	
Hurt	Understood	
Shame	Relieved	
Guilty	Accepted	
Remorseful	Honored	
Bored		
Confused		
Self-conscious		

Rule #2

Never Follow Words of Appreciation or Apology with a Conjunction

We learned about the power of gratitude in the last chapter. It is important to be careful not to cancel out positivity by immediately following a kind statement with a negative one. Therefore, try to end statements of appreciation, gratitude, and apology with a period. A simple, kind statement or compliment is the fastest and easiest way to remind your partner that you like them. If there is some negative or constructive feedback you'd like to give your partner, express that separately using the formula detailed in Chapter 5: How to Ask for What you Need.

Rule #2 Practice Worksheet
Joint Exercise

Instructions — *Work together to edit the statements below by removing the phrase that discounts the first statement. (See the Answer Key at the back of the book to check your work.)*

> ### Example
>
> **Original Statement:**
> I'm sorry I interrupted you, but I thought you were going to go on forever.
>
> **Edited Statement:**
> I'm sorry I interrupted you. , ~~but I thought you were going to go on forever~~.

1. You have a great sense of humor when you're not being sarcastic.

2. Thanks for trying to help, but you have no clue how to fold a load of laundry.

3. I'm sorry I raised my voice at you.

4. Thanks for helping me out with this email.

5. I'm sorry I'm late, but there was an accident on the highway.

6. I'm so proud of you for going back to the gym.

7. You are a great listener when you're not texting.

8. I really appreciate that you surprised me at work for lunch, but I'm still mad about the fight we had last night.

Rule #2 Practice Template
Independent Exercise: **Partner One**

Instructions Use the templates below to compliment, apologize, or thank your partner without following up with a conjunction.

1. Thank you for
....

2. I'm sorry about the time I
....

3. I'm so proud of you for
....

4. You look really cute when
....

5. It was a great idea when you
....

Now share your statements with your partner.

Rule #2 Practice Template
Independent Exercise: **Partner Two**

Instructions Use the templates below to compliment, apologize, or thank your partner without following up with a conjunction.

1. Thank you for
....

2. I'm sorry about the time I
....

3. I'm so proud of you for
....

4. You look really cute when
....

5. It was a great idea when you
....

 Now share your statements with your partner.

Rule #3

Use "I" Not "You" (Except Before a Compliment)

There is a reason your third-grade teacher taught you to use "I" statements. Using "I" rather than "you" decreases the likelihood that your statement will be perceived as an attack. It shows your partner that you are taking responsibility for your contribution instead of blaming them. When in doubt, use the first-person singular pronoun to start a difficult conversation.

Examples

Incorrect: *You* drive like a maniac.

Correct: *I* am feeling frightened.

Exception: You may start a sentence with the word "you" when it is followed by a compliment or another kind statement.

Example: *You* look amazing.

Rule #3 Practice Worksheet
Joint Exercise

Instructions *Work together to change the following statements from "you' to "I."*
(See the Answer Key for examples.)

1. YOU are so cheap.

Re-write: I

....

....

2. YOU burned the lasagna.

Re-write: I

....

3. YOU are 25 minutes late.

Re-write: I

....

4. YOU weren't even thinking of me when you decided to go out with your friends last night.

Re-write: I

....

....

5. YOU are wrong.

Re-write: I

....

....

6. YOU are my best friend.

Re-write: I

....

....

Rule #4

Avoid Run-On Sentences, Comma Splices, and Sentence Sprawls

It's important to use short, clear sentences if you want to be understood. Run-on sentences make it harder for your listener to empathize with you when you go on and on with numerous examples of how your partner is letting you down, and you'll lose their attention amongst all the details, which is much more likely to lead to feeling unheard and not listened to, and you might even think it's your listener's fault for being a bad listener instead of you working to try to be more concise in getting your ideas across. (See what I mean?)

Here is how to apply this concept in real life.

Example of **breaking** Rule #4

Carson: I'm feeling really frustrated right now because when I come home, the house is an absolute mess, and it was immaculate when I left, and you know this is really important to me because performing acts of service is my love language. Don't you remember we had a huge fight about this last week? It takes five seconds for you to forget everything you agreed to...

[Jamie feels confused]

Example of **following** Rule #4

Carson: Hey, babe, can you do me a favor and try to remember to pick up the clutter in the living room before dinner?

[Jamie feels clear about how to help]

Rule #4 Practice Worksheet
Joint Exercise

Work together to turn the following run-on sentences into concise statements. (See the Answer Key for sample answers.)

1. The way we divide housework is so unfair. I do everything around here. I get up at the crack of dawn, feed the dogs, make the coffee, and clean up the kitchen from last night's dinner even though we had agreed that was your chore since, of course, I'm the one who cooked, and yet I do it anyway and I never complain about it.

Re-write: I

....

....

....

2. I need you to talk about your feelings. You never talk to me. I've told you a million times that I want to know what's going through your head and what's on your mind, but yet you still don't do it. I know this comes from the way you were raised, and in your family no one ever talked about their emotions which, by the way, is why your sister drinks so much, as much as I hate to say it but it's the truth. I love you and I don't want to see this happen to you, and I'm right here and all you have to do is talk to me.

Re-write: I

....

....

....

3. I need you to stop criticizing me. You're always on my case and there are things you do that I don't like but I just let them slide because I don't want to argue with you but then it really gets on my nerves that I'm doing so much and yet all I hear is that I should be doing more. It's not fair and I'm really sick of it.

Re-write: I

....

....

....

Rule #5

Never Say "Never," "Always," or "Finally"

Certain words don't belong in a conversation with the love of your life. It's best to keep the words "never", "always" and "finally" out of your vocabulary entirely because these words will tempt your listener to find exceptions to what you're saying, instead of listening to your point of view.

Examples

Incorrect: You *never* consider my feelings.

Correct: I'm feeling left out.

Rule #5 Practice Worksheet

Joint Exercise

Instructions *Work together to circle the stop words in the sentences below. (See the Answer Key in the Appendix to check your work.)*

1. You always choose the TV show.

2. I'm so glad you finally learned how to make coffee.

3. Thanks for making coffee.

4. I never have any time to myself these days.

5. It seems to me we've been arguing more lately.

6. We always argue when we talk about finances.

7. Let's sit down and talk about our budget when we're both a little more well-rested.

8. I can't believe you finally remembered our anniversary without me hinting at it.

9. This has been the best anniversary celebration yet!

10. I heard about a new Netflix show I'd like to try out with you.

How to Follow These Rules in Real Life

Following all these rules is hard, especially when you are in the midst of a passionate or difficult conversation. You will break these rules sometimes and so will your partner. The best conversations will result when each of you is working to correct your mistakes and allowing yourselves time and space to mess up and keep practicing. You don't have to get it perfect; tweaking your language a little bit here and there can go a long way.

Talk to Each Other About the Ground Rules

Joint Exercise

Instructions *Take turns asking each other the questions below.*

1. Which of the 5 Ground Rules do you feel are strengths for you?

   1. Never place the word "that" or "like" after the words "I feel."

   2. Never follow words of appreciation or apology with a conjunction.

   3. Use "I" not "you" except before a compliment.

   4. Avoid run-on sentences, comma splices, and sentence sprawls.

   5. Never say "never," "always," or "finally."

2. Which of the 5 Ground Rules would you like to try to improve at following?

   1. Never place the word "that" or "like" after the words "I feel."

   2. Never follow words of appreciation or apology with a conjunction.

   3. Use "I" not "you" except before a compliment.

   4. Avoid run-on sentences, comma splices, and sentence sprawls.

   5. Never say "never," "always," or "finally."

3. How do you feel about these communication ground rules?

   1. I find these rules off-putting. I don't want to have to be so careful with how I talk to you.

   2. These rules make sense and are obvious to me, but I still have trouble following them.

   3. I like the structure of a concrete list of rules because it helps me stay focused.

   4. I already follow these rules consistently.

   5. I'm not sure how I feel about these rules.

4. Overall, how committed do you feel to following these communication rules in our relationship?

   1. Highly committed

   2. Somewhat committed

   3. Not at all committed

   4. Not sure

   5. Other . . . .

 # Chapter Review

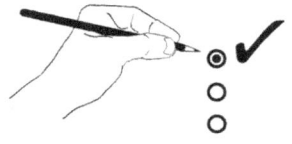

It doesn't only matter **what** you say, it matters **how** you say it.
Here's a recap of Laura's 5 Communication Ground Rules:

- Never place the word "that" or "like" after the words "I feel."

- Never follow words of appreciation or apology with a conjunction.

- Use "I" not "you" except before a compliment.

- Avoid run-on sentences, comma splices, and sentence sprawls.

- Never say "never," "always," or "finally."

 # Chapter Challenge

In the next day or two, listen closely to dialogues on podcasts, TV shows, or movies. See if you can spot examples of people breaking these communication rules. Notice how the conversations progress.

Now that you have some core ground rules under your belt, we'll be taking a deeper dive into conflict management.

"What people often mean by getting rid of conflict is getting rid of diversity, and it is of the utmost importance that these should not be considered the same... Fear of difference is dread of life itself." [1]

Mary Parker-Follett

Chapter 4
How to Deal With Conflict
Three productive ways to manage differences

You can avoid a fight, as discussed in Chapter 3, but it's impossible to avoid conflict altogether. Conflict is a process of integrating differences, and 100% of couples have differences of opinion. In other words, you can have conflict without arguing, but you can't have a relationship without conflict.

Although conflict is a normal and natural part of all relationships, there is immense variation in how couples deal with differences. Sadly, toxicity and abuse can sometimes result in couples' inability to manage differences in a healthy manner. (Reminder: If you believe you may be in an abusive relationship, seek help from a licensed professional.)

Conflict is not intrinsically bad. When differences are integrated productively, couples learn and grow together. Strong conflict management skills allow people to solve difficult problems, make life-changing decisions, and expand their understanding of complex issues. Take the Conflict True or False Quiz on the next page to reflect on your feelings about confrontation.

Conflict True or False Quiz
Independent Exercise: **Partner One**

Instructions — *Answer the following true or false questions. This exercise is for self-reflection purposes only. There are no right or wrong answers.*

1. I detest confrontation.

   Very True ○ ○ ○ ○ ○ *Very False*
           1   2   3   4   5

2. I can't stand it when I know something's up but no one is talking about the elephant in the room.

   Very True ○ ○ ○ ○ ○ *Very False*
           1   2   3   4   5

3. I often don't want to talk about things because I know it will turn into a fight and people's feelings will get hurt.

   Very True ○ ○ ○ ○ ○ *Very False*
           1   2   3   4   5

4. My partner usually wants to keep talking when things get a little heated, whereas I tend to want some space.

   Very True ○ ○ ○ ○ ○ *Very False*
           1   2   3   4   5

5. I usually want to keep talking when things get a little heated, whereas my partner tends to want some space.

   Very True ○ ○ ○ ○ ○ *Very False*
           1   2   3   4   5

6. I feel closer when people tell me their true feelings, even when they are negative.

   Very True ○ ○ ○ ○ ○ *Very False*
           1   2   3   4   5

7. I believe in the philosophy, "If you don't have anything nice to say, don't say anything at all."

   Very True ○ ○ ○ ○ ○ *Very False*
           1   2   3   4   5

8. I prefer a lively debate over small talk.

   Very True ○ ○ ○ ○ ○ *Very False*
           1   2   3   4   5

♡
Share your responses and insights with your partner after each of you has completed your quiz.

Conflict True or False Quiz
Independent Exercise: *Partner Two*

Instructions *Answer the following true or false questions. This exercise is for self-reflection purposes only. There are no right or wrong answers.*

1. I detest confrontation.

   Very True   O   O   O   O   O   Very False
               1   2   3   4   5

2. I can't stand it when I know something's up but no one is talking about the elephant in the room.

   Very True   O   O   O   O   O   Very False
               1   2   3   4   5

3. I often don't want to talk about things because I know it will turn into a fight and people's feelings will get hurt.

   Very True   O   O   O   O   O   Very False
               1   2   3   4   5

4. My partner usually wants to keep talking when things get a little heated, whereas I tend to want some space.

   Very True   O   O   O   O   O   Very False
               1   2   3   4   5

5. I usually want to keep talking when things get a little heated, whereas my partner tends to want some space.

   Very True   O   O   O   O   O   Very False
               1   2   3   4   5

6. I feel closer when people tell me their true feelings, even when they are negative.

   Very True   O   O   O   O   O   Very False
               1   2   3   4   5

7. I believe in the philosophy, "If you don't have anything nice to say, don't say anything at all."

   Very True   O   O   O   O   O   Very False
               1   2   3   4   5

8. I prefer a lively debate over small talk.

   Very True   O   O   O   O   O   Very False
               1   2   3   4   5

Share your responses and insights with your partner after each of you has completed your quiz.

The 5 Different Conflict Management Styles

The Gottmans' research[2] suggests that there are five distinct conflict management styles. Two are dysfunctional approaches and three are functional. John Gottman uses the terms below to classify them:

2 Dysfunctional Conflict Styles

- **Hostile Couples** display contempt, criticism, and defensiveness, and make little effort to understand the other's point of view.

- **Hostile-Detached Couples** display high levels of shut-down and resignation, often resulting in a bitter stalemate.

> I have created an interactive quiz called "What's Your Conflict Style?"
> which you can take on my website by following this link:
> https://laurasilverstein.co/conflict-quiz.

Thankfully, hostile-detached couples can turn things around by learning and practicing emotional regulation and communication skills.

The remainder of this chapter will explore the three functional conflict management styles. You might think that one of these three approaches is better than the others but, in fact, all three work.

3 Functional Conflict Styles

- **Validating Couples** show high levels of empathy and value, seeing both sides of an issue. They tend to modulate their emotions during discussions.

- **Conflict-Avoiding Couples** prefer to focus on similarities instead of differences and tend to avoid high levels of emotional intensity.

- **Volatile Couples** don't shy away from differences and instead discuss them with a high level of passion, humor, and honesty.[2]

As you learn about the three functional styles, you may feel that one or more have a negative connotation. This might be due to the labels chosen to describe the styles, or it may be because you highly value one style over the other two. The three functional styles can become hostile if the disagreements escalate to the point where negativity outweighs positivity and neither person accepts the other's attempts to de-escalate. (See Chapter 2 to understand the importance of positivity in relationships, and Chapter 7 to learn how to take a break to avoid conflict toxicity.)

Preferred Conflict Styles

Here are the three functional conflict styles in more depth:

1. Validating

People with validating conflict styles like to hear all points of view. They value equality and empathy, and are comfortable with emotional expression as long as it is relatively contained. Differences of opinion are seen as opportunities for compromise and understanding.

Advantages: This style is effective for compromise, deep understanding, and emotional intimacy. People who prefer the Validating style tend to be willing to put the time in to make sure all parties in the conversation feel understood.

Disadvantages: Even though this style seems ideal, it is the most time-consuming of all three styles and there is a risk of couples wasting time over-processing their relationship and re-hashing things that would be better put to rest. Sometimes it's wise to bite your tongue even when your feelings are hurt.

2. Conflict Avoiding

People who prefer a Conflict Avoiding style like to keep the peace and avoid drama. They value kindness and prefer to bite their tongue when possible, avoiding what they might consider "brutal honesty." Differences of opinion are accepted and respected, with limited attempts to persuade the other to change their mind.

Advantages: This style is effective at avoiding unnecessary drama. Emotions are kept light, which tends to contribute to a calmer and more peaceful environment.

Disadvantages: Too much conflict avoidance can potentially build resentment if issues are never raised at all. With less direct communication, couples can experience anxiety wondering what their partner is thinking or feeling about them.

3. Volatile

People who prefer a Volatile conflict style don't shy away from intense emotion. They speak their minds, value passion and honesty, and enjoy lively debate. Volatile couples differ from the dysfunctional hostile style as there is evidence of tenderness and hearty humor during interactions. Differences of opinion are seen as opportunities to learn and grow.

Advantages: The advantage of a Volatile conflict management style is that everyone acknowledges the "elephant in the room" which leads to increased trust and authenticity. No one walks away wondering what the other person is thinking. Conversations are intimate and full of passion.

Disadvantages: One of the potential drawbacks of the Volatile conflict style is that banter and teasing can go too far, resulting in hurt feelings. Couples can become so caught up with what they are saying that they stop listening to each other.

NOTE: People are rarely limited to only one style, and preferences change over time and according to context.

Conflict Style
Conversation Starter
Joint Exercise

Instructions *Take turns asking your partner the questions below to discuss your thoughts on the three functional conflict styles.*

1. Based on the descriptions above, which conflict style do you tend to prefer most of the time?

     1. Validating

     2. Conflict Avoiding

     3. Volatile

     4. A combination of .... and ....

     5. Not sure

2. What are your thoughts about the three conflict styles?

3. How do you think our preferred conflict styles play out in our relationship?

If you and your partner share the same preferred conflict style, you are less likely to have what I call "conflict conflict," that is to say arguments about the right or wrong way to express differences. It will be helpful to remember that these three styles are all functional.

If you and your partner have different preferred conflict styles, it might be a bit more difficult to find a way to manage differences in the short term but, in the long run, you'll better understand the benefits of your partner's approach and vice versa. This may also help you in contexts outside your relationship when you are talking to people with different preferred conflict styles.

Deciding When to Bring Things Up and When to Let them Slide

A large part of conflict management includes deciding *if*, *when*, and *how* to raise an issue. In the next chapters, we'll detail *how* to talk about difficult topics – but first, it's important to determine *whether to bring up the topic at all*.

You only have two options when it comes to deciding what to do when an issue arises:

1. Let it slide

2. Talk it out (now or later)

Here are my recommendations regarding the criteria to use when deciding which option to choose.

When to Let Things Slide

1. When You're Irritable

The worst time to start a conversation is when you're already in a bad mood. If you are having the kind of day when you're feeling irritable and nothing is going right, it's not a good time to start a difficult conversation with your partner. Instead, I recommend some self-care. Go for a walk, listen to your favorite music, or find an animal to pet.

2. When It's an Issue You Are Already Working to Fix

Let things slide when the issue is an ongoing work in progress. If your partner is working hard to correct something that you have brought to their attention but slides back a bit, give them a chance to self-correct or independently apologize. You don't want to add insult to injury by expressing irritation when they feel bad for letting you down and are motivated to improve.

When Not to Let Things Slide

If you are upset about something for multiple days and the topic doesn't fit into one of the two above categories, it probably means it's worth speaking up.

Talk it Out or Let it Slide
Practice Worksheet
Joint Exercise

Work together to decide whether to talk it out or let it slide. Think about each scenario below. Based on the advice above, indicate whether I (Laura, the author of this Workbook!) would recommend talking it out or letting it slide? (See the Answer Key.)

1. You had a terrible night's sleep and wake up feeling physically, mentally, and emotionally exhausted. As you're heading for the coffee maker, you step in dog pee because your partner forgot to take your puppy out last night. You are tempted to run upstairs and wake up your partner to let them have it. What would I suggest?

        A. Let it slide

        B. Talk it out

2. You and your partner are alone in the car on a 3-hour road trip for a long weekend away. You're both happy and relaxed. Your partner asks you how you're doing because they've noticed you seem tense lately. Your partner hurt your feelings a few days ago and it's still lingering. What would I suggest?

        A. Let it slide

        B. Talk it out

3. . Your partner is running late and very stressed out about a lunch meeting with an estranged relative. You're trying to help, but your partner is terse with you and apologizes quickly. You didn't feel the apology was sincere. What would I suggest?

        A. Let it slide

        B. Talk it out

4. You and your partner are on your way to a wedding and there is a car accident ahead of you on the road so you're not sure if you'll make it on time. You had already mentioned you should probably leave earlier and are tempted to remind your partner that it wouldn't be so stressful if they had been ready to leave 15 minutes earlier. What would I suggest?

        A. Let it slide

        B. Talk it out

5. Your partner is upset about an argument you had last night and sits down to tell you how they're feeling. You would rather catch up on your emails like you were planning, but you've got nothing urgent to do at the moment.

        A. Let it slide

        B. Talk it out

Conflict Management Conversation Starter

Joint Exercise

Instructions ❯ *Take turns asking each other the questions below.*

1. Do you agree with Laura's recommendations about when to talk it out and when to let things slide? Why or why not?

2. Overall, do you wish I spoke up more or less about my frustrations or disagreements?

3. What do you want me to understand about how you feel during our conflicts?

4. In our relationship, do you think we err more on the side of over-processing or avoiding conflict too much?

5. What do you think is working well regarding how we currently manage conflict?

 # Chapter Review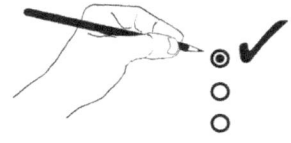

There are five different conflict styles for how people prefer to manage differences. Two of these styles (Hostile and Hostile-Avoidant) are dysfunctional, and three (Validating, Avoiding, and Volatile) are functional as long as there is a higher proportion of positivity to negativity. Within these styles are also differences about when to talk a topic out, and when to let it slide.

The more time you devote to understanding how you and your partner's conflict management styles and preferences intersect, the less likely you are to have "conflict conflict."

 # Chapter Challenge

I have an interactive quiz set up on my website to help you learn more about your specific conflict style. Take my interactive quiz, "What's Your Conflict Style?" here:

https://laurasilverstein.co/conflict-quiz/

Now that you understand your conflict styles and preferences, you'll need specific tools and strategies for what to say (and what not to say) when significant differences arise. The next three chapters will provide you with tools, flowcharts and conversation starters. We'll start by addressing how to ask for what you need.

*"Ask for what you want
and be prepared to get it."*[1]

Maya Angelou

Chapter 5
How to Ask for What You Need
Without sounding critical

The best way to get what you need is to ask for it (even though "you might wish you didn't have to say it"). You are worthy and deserve to have your needs heard. This chapter addresses how to speak your truth, raise difficult conversations, and provide constructive feedback.

We can make the mistake of staying silent and putting our partner's needs before our own, and we can also make the mistake of speaking our truth with so much intensity that we put our own needs before our partner's. It can be hard to create balance in your relationship such that both of you are in the habit of speaking up about what you want and need, while also working to give your partner what they need and want. This chapter will focus on *how* to ask for what you need and in the next chapter you'll learn how to focus on giving your partner what they are asking for.

Negative communication cycles happen when couples forget to choose their words mindfully and thoughtfully. While it is crucial to speak your truth, it is equally as important to do so with kindness and respect.

Asking for What I Need
True or False Self-Reflection Quiz
Independent Exercise: **Partner One**

Instructions ▶ *Answer the following true or false questions. This exercise is for self-reflection purposes only. There are no right or wrong answers.*

1. It is hard for me to ask for what I need.

    Very True ○   ○   ○   ○   ○   Very False
              1   2   3   4   5

2. It is a strength of mine to ask for what I need.

    Very True ○   ○   ○   ○   ○   Very False
              1   2   3   4   5

3. Sometimes I find myself waiting too long to ask for what I need, so when I finally do, it comes out with a sharp edge.

    Very True ○   ○   ○   ○   ○   Very False
              1   2   3   4   5

4. Sometimes I am so focused on asking for what I need that I don't consider my partner when I'm speaking.

    Very True ○   ○   ○   ○   ○   Very False
              1   2   3   4   5

5. I can be a people-pleaser and stay silent about my needs even when my feelings about the issue are very strong.

    Very True ○   ○   ○   ○   ○   Very False
              1   2   3   4   5

6. I can be overly critical of my partner.

    Very True ○   ○   ○   ○   ○   Very False
              1   2   3   4   5

8. I believe that it is my responsibility to speak my truth with kindness and respect, even when I am upset or angry.

    Very True ○   ○   ○   ○   ○   Very False
              1   2   3   4   5

10. I want to work together to find a better way for both of us to ask for what we need.

    Very True ○   ○   ○   ○   ○   Very False
              1   2   3   4   5

♡ Share your responses and insights with your partner after each of you has completed your quiz.

Asking for What I Need
True or False Self-Reflection Quiz
Independent Exercise: *Partner Two*

Instructions *Answer the following true or false questions. This exercise is for self-reflection purposes only. There are no right or wrong answers.*

1. It is hard for me to ask for what I need.

    Very True   O   O   O   O   O   Very False
               1   2   3   4   5

2. It is a strength of mine to ask for what I need.

    Very True   O   O   O   O   O   Very False
               1   2   3   4   5

3. Sometimes I find myself waiting too long to ask for what I need, so when I finally do, it comes out with a sharp edge.

    Very True   O   O   O   O   O   Very False
               1   2   3   4   5

4. Sometimes I am so focused on asking for what I need that I don't consider my partner when I'm speaking.

    Very True   O   O   O   O   O   Very False
               1   2   3   4   5

5. I can be a people-pleaser and stay silent about my needs even when my feelings about the issue are very strong.

    Very True   O   O   O   O   O   Very False
               1   2   3   4   5

6. I can be overly critical of my partner.

    Very True   O   O   O   O   O   Very False
               1   2   3   4   5

8. I believe that it is my responsibility to speak my truth with kindness and respect, even when I am upset or angry.

    Very True   O   O   O   O   O   Very False
               1   2   3   4   5

10. I want to work together to find a better way for both of us to ask for what we need.

    Very True   O   O   O   O   O   Very False
               1   2   3   4   5

Share your responses and insights with your partner after each of you has completed your quiz.

How to Prevent the Attack-Defend Cycle
The Attack-Defend Cycle

In order to understand how to have productive conversations, it is important to understand what leads to counter-productive dialogues so that you can recognize the red flags and avoid them. The most common dysfunctional communication pattern is an attack-defend cycle.[2] Here is how the pattern plays out:

1. You gather the confidence to speak up and ask for what you need.

2. Your partner feels hurt or attacked (even though this wasn't your intention).

3. Your partner responds defensively.

4. You feel dismissed (even though this wasn't their intention).

5. You amplify the volume or intensity in articulating your need.

6. The cycle repeats.

Opposite is a visual representation
As you can see in the diagram, raising a topic in a critical manner will likely lead to a defensive response and an escalation of the attack-defend cycle.

The Attack-Defend Cycle

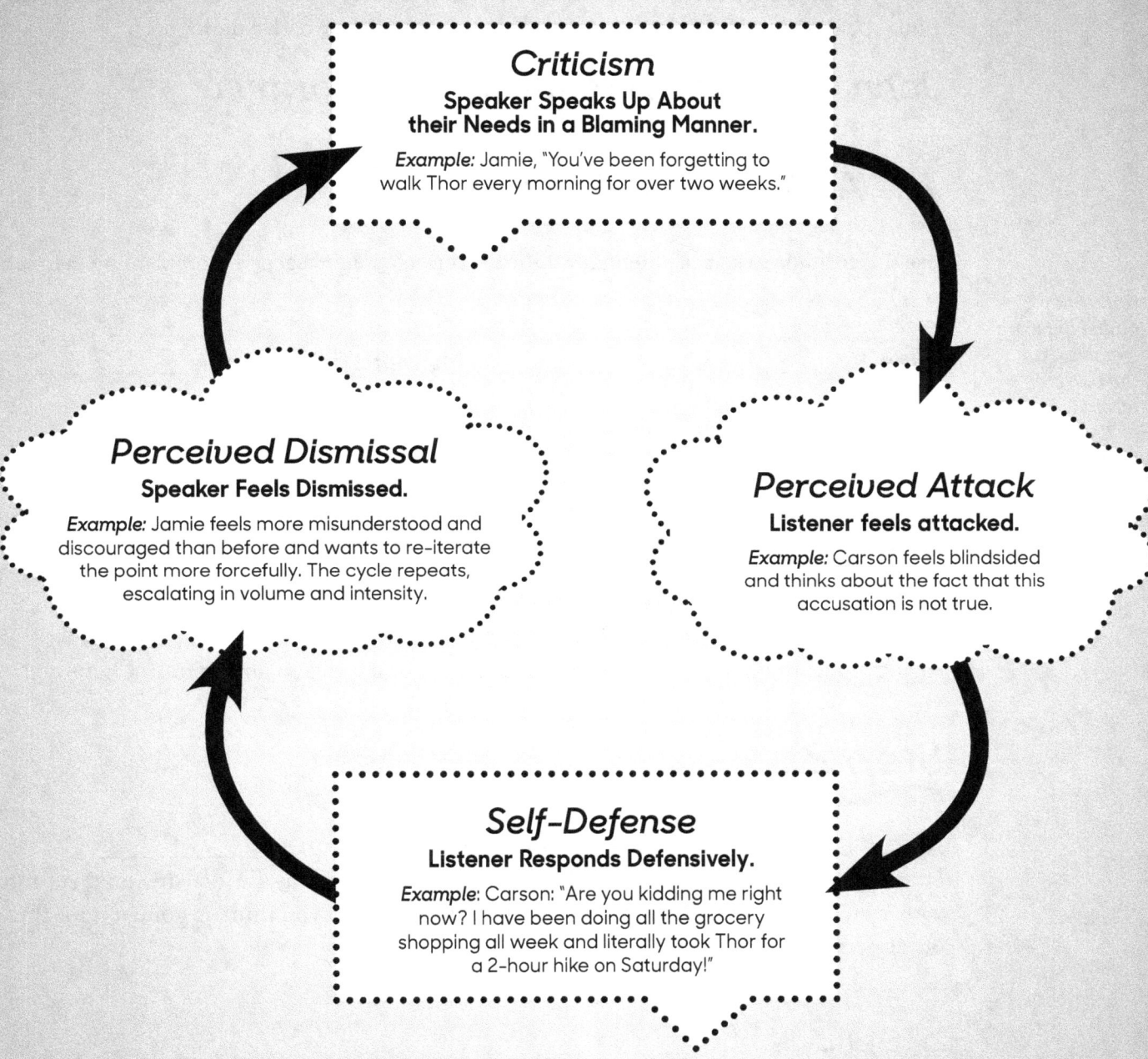

Criticism
Speaker Speaks Up About their Needs in a Blaming Manner.

Example: Jamie, "You've been forgetting to walk Thor every morning for over two weeks."

Perceived Attack
Listener feels attacked.

Example: Carson feels blindsided and thinks about the fact that this accusation is not true.

Self-Defense
Listener Responds Defensively.

Example: Carson: "Are you kidding me right now? I have been doing all the grocery shopping all week and literally took Thor for a 2-hour hike on Saturday!"

Perceived Dismissal
Speaker Feels Dismissed.

Example: Jamie feels more misunderstood and discouraged than before and wants to re-iterate the point more forcefully. The cycle repeats, escalating in volume and intensity.

Why Most Communication Skills Training Fails

Communication skills training usually fails because it has historically focused on *listening* skills instead of *speaking* skills. This is too bad because many well-meaning couples blame themselves when they follow active listening advice and it doesn't work. Both speaking *and* listening are crucial elements of a productive dialogue.

John Gottman's Gentle Startup Formula[3]

The Antidote to Criticism

Use this formula to start a potentially difficult conversation in a gentle, non-blaming manner:

Note: *I have added the word "request" to the Gottman's formula [3] as I have found it to be effective with the couples I serve.*

"I feel _____ about _____ My need or request is _____"

Here is how to fill in the blanks to get the best results.

Step 1

"I feel _____ (state emotion) _____"

Begin your statements with "I" instead of "You" to avoid placing blame, and avoid saying "I feel that" or "I feel like" (see Laura's Ground Rules #1 and #3 from Chapter 3).

Step 2

"about _____ (the situation not the person) _____"

Describe what is happening, objectively and non-judgmentally, by focusing on facts and your own perceptions. Don't offer your evaluation of what you think is going on for the other person.

Step 3

"My need or request is _____ (concrete behavioral request) _____"

Your message will be best received when you talk about what you need or want in clear and positive terms. Be specific and explicit, clarifying what you *do* want rather than what you *don't* want.

Step 4

Integrate appreciation and manners

Express appreciation. Even when you are giving negative feedback, I recommend taking the time to remember an occasion when your partner met your needs. It will help them feel understood and more willing to hear your perspective when you can show them that their efforts and strengths have not gone unnoticed.

Remember to be polite, and use phrases such as "please" and "I would appreciate it if." Challenge your belief that this person "always or never" does the thing in question.

Here are some Gentle Startup examples:

I feel disappointed about the frequency of our love-making. I appreciate how hard it is to risk rejection, but I'd like you to try to initiate affection more often.

I feel frustrated when there are dirty dishes on the counter in the morning when I had cleaned the kitchen before going to bed. I know how much you hate doing dishes, and I want to decide on a way to fairly share chores.

I feel dismissed when I am interrupted. I appreciate how passionate you are and love hearing your ideas. Please listen to what I'm saying before adding your own ideas.

Gentle Startup Practice Worksheet

Joint Exercise

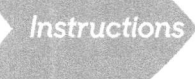

Instructions Work together as a team to turn each example of a criticism into a gentle startup using the guidelines below. Check the answer key for the author's responses, keeping in mind that there are multiple ways to complete this exercise effectively.

1. "You're always late for dinner and you never think about anyone but yourself."

I feel _____ about or when _____

_____

My need or request is _____

_____

2. "You are so careless when you load the dishwasher and don't even seem to care whether my mother's china gets cracked."

I feel _____ about or when _____

_____

My need or request is _____

_____

3. "You are always nagging me and it doesn't matter what I do because you're going to find something wrong with it, so why should I even bother?"

I feel _____ about or when _____

_____

My need or request is _____

_____

4. "You're not the only one around here who works hard."

I feel _____ about or when _____

_____

My need or request is _____

_____

5. "If you keep spending money at this rate we won't be able to pay our rent. And there is absolutely no way I'm moving back in with your parents."

I feel _____ *about or when* _____

_____

My need or request is _____

_____

6. "You never listen to me."

I feel _____ *about or when* _____

_____

My need or request is _____

_____

7. "You always say no when I initiate love-making."

I feel _____ *about or when* _____

_____

My need or request is _____

_____

8. "Your job is more important to you than your marriage."

I feel _____ *about or when* _____

_____

My need or request is _____

_____

Ask for What You Need Template

Independent Exercise: **Partner One**

> **Instructions** Use the space below to craft a gentle startup for a real issue in your relationship.

TIP: For skill development, it is recommended to choose something real, but not your biggest issue or something that has a highly charged history. Some examples might be differences in cleanliness, tardiness, or day to day annoyances. For now, avoid topics such as differences in religion, parenting, or issues related to trauma, substance abuse, or mental illness.

I feel _____ about or when _____

_____

My need or request is _____

_____

Tips For Success

As you're practicing the Gentle Startup formula, note that there are some things to avoid:

• Don't sound like a robot. Remember tone of voice matters.

• Remember to follow your "I" statement with your request.

• Follow the word "feel" with an emotion, rather than "like" or "that".
(Laura's Ground Rule #1)

The earlier you speak up about the thing that is bothering you, the easier it will be to follow this advice. You won't have the compounding frustration that builds when you silently suffer.

Ask for What You Need Template

Independent Exercise: **Partner Two**

Instructions *Use the space below to craft a gentle startup for a real issue in your relationship.*

TIP: For skill development, it is recommended to choose something real, but not your biggest issue or something that has a highly charged history. Some examples might be differences in cleanliness, tardiness, or day to day annoyances. For now, avoid topics such as differences in religion, parenting, or issues related to trauma, substance abuse, or mental illness.

I feel _____ about or when _____

_____

My need or request is _____

_____

Tips For Success

As you're practicing the Gentle Startup formula, note that there are some things to avoid:

- Don't sound like a robot. Remember tone of voice matters.

- Remember to follow your "I" statement with your request.

- Follow the word "feel" with an emotion, rather than "like" or "that".
(Laura's Ground Rule #1)

The earlier you speak up about the thing that is bothering you, the easier it will be to follow this advice. You won't have the compounding frustration that builds when you silently suffer.

Share Your Gentle Startups
Joint Exercise

Instructions  *Take turns reading your Gentle Startups to each other. Use the space below to make notes. Then thank your partner for sharing their feelings, but DO NOT CONTINUE THE CONVERSATION AT THIS TIME.*

....

....

....

....

....

Thank you so much for letting me know how you feel. Let's keep talking about this later.

Resist the urge to keep talking about this topic. Now that you know how to start a conversation, the next chapter will address how to respond to a request without getting sucked inot the attack-defend cycle.

Chapter Review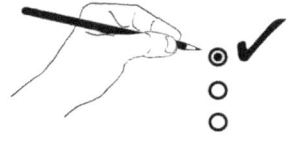

It's crucial to speak up about what you want and need. Not speaking up might lead to resentment, which could come out sideways. When you are ready to express yourself to your partner, the way you begin the conversation will determine how the dialogue progresses. By using a Gentle Startup, you are more likely to avoid the very common and extremely frustrating attack-defend communication cycle. Constructive conversations move forward instead of in a circle.

Here is a review of the formula:

I feel _____ about _____ My need or request is _____

Chapter Challenge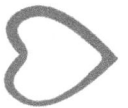

Find an opportunity to offer another gentle startup by the end of the day tomorrow. Start by asking, "Is now a good time for me to practice another gentle startup?

Now that you know how to start a conversation clearly and respectfully, the next chapter will address how to respond to your partner's requests without getting sucked into an attack-defend cycle.

"Criticism is something we can avoid easily by saying nothing, doing nothing, and being nothing."

Unknown

Chapter 6
How to Respond to Criticism
Without sounding defensive

*I'm sure you know what it's like to feel blamed, judged, chastised, or critiqued. Even though you probably value constructive feedback, you don't want it to be rubbed in your face or expressed to you in a critical or patronizing way. No matter how it is delivered, it is still important to have a way to respond to negative feedback. I said earlier that the onus of responsibility for a productive conversation lies on the speaker **and** the listener. This chapter is about what to do when your partner asks for what they need in a critical way.*

What is Criticism?
Criticism, by definition[1], is a statement that implies that there is something fundamentally wrong with someone or something. Criticism gives the impression the problem exists in the person, not the mistake that was made. This chapter will address how to respond to criticism so that you can get out of an attack-defend or attack-counter-attack communication pattern.

Responding to Criticism
True or False Quiz

Independent Exercise: Partner One

Instructions ▸ *Answer the following true or false questions. This exercise is for self-reflection purposes only. There are no right or wrong answers.*

1. Even though it's hard to hear, I want my partner to speak up about their needs.

   Very True ○ ○ ○ ○ ○ *Very False*
          1 2 3 4 5

2. When my partner tells me I've let them down, I get angry pretty quickly and think of all the things my partner does to me that I never bring up.

   Very True ○ ○ ○ ○ ○ *Very False*
          1 2 3 4 5

3. I'm pretty good at saying, "I'm sorry" when my partner gives me feedback.

   Very True ○ ○ ○ ○ ○ *Very False*
          1 2 3 4 5

4. One of my biggest triggers is when I feel unjustly accused.

   Very True ○ ○ ○ ○ ○ *Very False*
          1 2 3 4 5

5. I try to take my partner's feedback seriously and do my best to give them what they are asking for.

   Very True ○ ○ ○ ○ ○ *Very False*
          1 2 3 4 5

6. I can be overly sensitive to criticism.

   Very True ○ ○ ○ ○ ○ *Very False*
          1 2 3 4 5

7. It is a strength of mine to take accountability for my part in a problem.

   Very True ○ ○ ○ ○ ○ *Very False*
          1 2 3 4 5

8. I want to learn how to respond to criticism because sometimes I can get defensive.

   Very True ○ ○ ○ ○ ○ *Very False*
          1 2 3 4 5

Share your responses and insights with your partner after each of you has completed your quiz.

Responding to Criticism
True or False Quiz
Independent Exercise: **Partner Two**

Instructions *Answer the following true or false questions. This exercise is for self-reflection purposes only. There are no right or wrong answers.*

1. Even though it's hard to hear, I want my partner to speak up about their needs.

Very True   O   O   O   O   O   *Very False*
        1   2   3   4   5

2. When my partner tells me I've let them down, I get angry pretty quickly and think of all the things my partner does to me that I never bring up.

Very True   O   O   O   O   O   *Very False*
        1   2   3   4   5

3. I'm pretty good at saying, "I'm sorry" when my partner gives me feedback.

Very True   O   O   O   O   O   *Very False*
        1   2   3   4   5

4. One of my biggest triggers is when I feel unjustly accused.

Very True   O   O   O   O   O   *Very False*
        1   2   3   4   5

5. I try to take my partner's feedback seriously and do my best to give them what they are asking for.

Very True   O   O   O   O   O   *Very False*
        1   2   3   4   5

6. I can be overly sensitive to criticism.

Very True   O   O   O   O   O   *Very False*
        1   2   3   4   5

Share your responses and insights with your partner after each of you has completed your quiz.

7. It is a strength of mine to take accountability for my part in a problem.

Very True   O   O   O   O   O   *Very False*
        1   2   3   4   5

8. I want to learn how to respond to criticism because sometimes I can get defensive.

Very True   O   O   O   O   O   *Very False*
        1   2   3   4   5

How to Respond to Criticism

*It is normal to feel pulled into defensiveness when someone blames you. You'll want to explain your innocence, set the record straight, and explain the misunderstanding. Perhaps you hope that as soon as you clarify **why** you did or said what you did, your partner will understand your perspective and the problem will be quickly resolved.*

Although it's common knowledge that criticism is negative, many people don't know that responding with defensiveness is just as problematic. Self-defense is the very thing that keeps the negative communication pattern repeating, and leading to long, frustrating, counter-productive conversations, as you can see on the Attack-Defend Cycle Illustration on the next page.

Here is how the attack-defend cycle plays out when you are the listener:

1. Your partner speaks up asking for what they need.

2. You feel hurt or attacked (even if it wasn't your partner's intention to hurt you).

3. You defend yourself (by explaining your innocence, providing additional information about why you did what you did, or reminding your partner of times when they have let you down).

4. Your partner feels dismissed (even though you intended to help them understand).

5. Your partner amplifies the volume or intensity of their feedback.

6. The cycle repeats.

The Attack-Defend Cycle

Criticism
Speaker Speaks Up About their Needs in a Blaming Manner.

Example: Jamie, "You've been forgetting to walk Thor every morning for over two weeks."

Perceived Attack
Listener feels attacked.

Example: Carson feels blindsided and thinks about the fact that this accusation is not true.

Self-Defense
Listener Responds Defensively.

Example: Carson: "Are you kidding me right now? I have been doing all the grocery shopping all week and literally took Thor for a 2-hour hike on Saturday!"

Perceived Dismissal
Speaker Feels Dismissed.

Example: Jamie feels more misunderstood and discouraged than before and wants to re-iterate the point with an increase intensity. The cycle repeats, escalating in volume and intensity.

Escape the Attack-Defend Cycle by Taking Accountability

Defending oneself when feeling attacked is not the only option. The attack-defend cycle can be broken by responding to criticism non-defensively. The Gottmans' research shows that taking accountability is the best alternative to defensiveness. This is done by admitting to a kernel of truth in what your partner is saying when you're feeling unjustly accused. The communication goal is to transform the circular cycle into a linear one. See the images on the next page

Here is what happens when someone takes accountability when feeling criticized:

> Carson: You're late.
>
> Jamie: I know. I'm so sorry. I know you told me you needed the car for your appointment, and you wanted me to show up early, not 5 minutes late.

6 Quick Tips for Taking Accountability

1. **Be specific**

   Instead of saying, "I'm sorry I hurt your feelings," say "I'm sorry I was insensitive in making a joke that was hurtful to you and not at all funny."

2. **Dig deep for agreement**

   When you're feeling criticized it's natural to point out what your partner got wrong. Try to find at least one small thing you agree with, and start with that.

3. **Slow down**

   Attack-defend cycles escalate quickly. When you feel the energy rising, take a breath first before responding reactively.

4. **Remember intent**

   Your partner probably isn't criticizing you to make you feel bad. They are raising an issue that is important to them in an effort to be honest and vulnerable.

5. **Set your pride aside**

   Apologizing can be hard because it can feel like admitting defeat. In truth, accepting responsibility will lead to **connecting** instead of **winning or losing**. You both are on the same team.

6. **Allow yourselves some grace**

   You are two people doing the best you can to co-create a happy, healthy relationship. When you remember you are both going to mess up sometimes, it can be easier to acknowledge your contribution to the problems (and the solution).

How to *Escape* the Attack-Defend Cycle

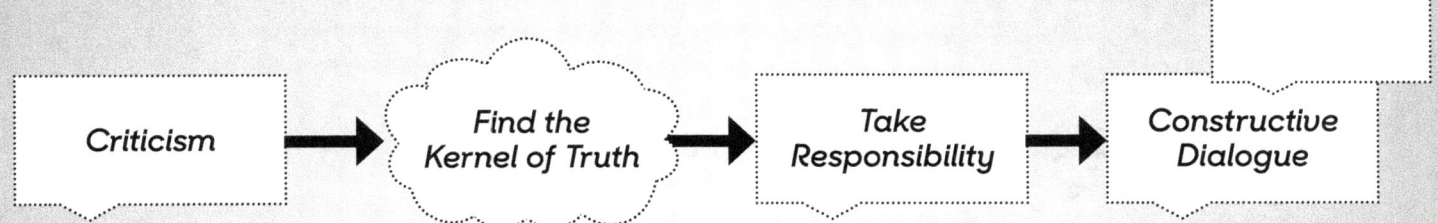

Criticism → Find the Kernel of Truth → Take Responsibility → Constructive Dialogue

Example

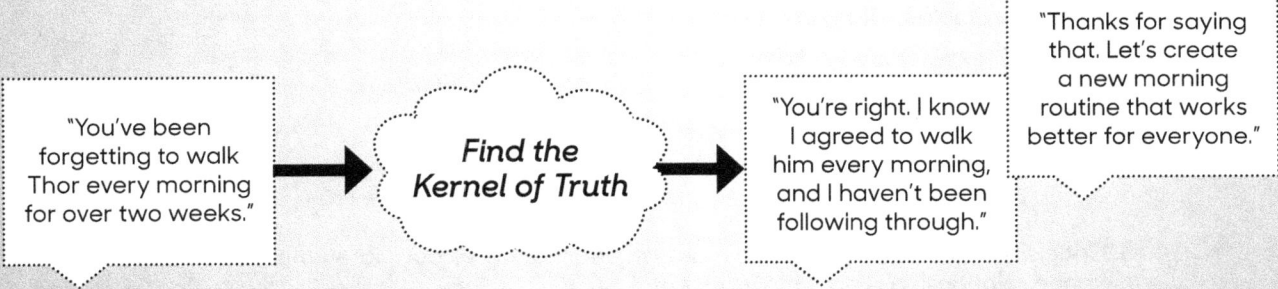

"You've been forgetting to walk Thor every morning for over two weeks." → Find the Kernel of Truth → "You're right. I know I agreed to walk him every morning, and I haven't been following through." → "Thanks for saying that. Let's create a new morning routine that works better for everyone."

Accountability Practice Worksheet

Joint Exercise

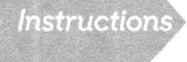

Instructions ▸ *Work as a team to craft a non-defensive response to the examples of criticism below. See the answer key for examples.*

1. Criticism: "You are irresponsible with money."
Example of taking accountability:

....

....

2. Criticism: "You're not even listening to me."
Example of taking accountability:

....

....

3. Criticism: "You used to text me all the time and now I hardly ever hear from you anymore."
Example of taking accountability:

....

....

4. Criticism: "You're driving like a maniac!"
Example of taking accountability:

....

....

5. Criticism: "You're gonna have to make an effort to carve out more time for me if this long-distance relationship is going to work out."
Example of taking accountability:

....

....

6. Criticism: "You think you're a better parent than me, but you're not."
Example of taking accountability:

....

....

Craft Your Real-Life Apology
Independent Exercise: **Partner One**

Instructions *Think of something that you are ready to apologize about. It doesn't need to be a big thing, but it does need to be a real thing. Use the space provided to practice taking accountability for a real-world issue. Use your own language or the prompts to guide you and then share your apology with your partner. DO NOT KEEP TALKING ABOUT THE ISSUE at this time. Simply thank each other and move on.*

Example

I recognize that I hurt or disappointed you when I rolled my eyes while you were talking. Even though I felt defensive, I see your point of view and I'm sorry.

I recognize that I hurt or disappointed you when I

....

Even though I felt defensive, I see your point of view and I'm sorry.

Craft Your Apology
for a Real-World Issue
Independent Exercise: **Partner Two**

Instructions *Think of something that you are ready to apologize about. It doesn't need to be a big thing, but it does need to be a real thing. Use the space provided to practice taking accountability for a real-world issue. Use your own language or the prompts to guide you and then share your apology with your partner. DO NOT KEEP TALKING ABOUT THE ISSUE at this time. Simply thank each other and move on.*

Example

I recognize that I hurt or disappointed you when I rolled my eyes while you were talking. Even though I felt defensive, I see your point of view and I'm sorry.

I recognize that I hurt or disappointed you when I

....

Even though I felt defensive, I see your point of view and I'm sorry.

10 Ways to Say Sorry

1. I recognize that I hurt or disappointed you when I _____.
   Even though I felt defensive, I see your point of view and I'm sorry.

2. I could have done a better job with _____ and I'll keep working on this.

3. I'm really sorry I _____.

4. I know I've been _____ lately even though you've asked me not to.

5. I know I forgot to _____ even though I agreed to do it. That's on me.

6. Sorry I sounded defensive when you let me know I _____.
   You were right, even though it was hard to hear.

7. I got it wrong when I _____, and I'll try to make it right.

8. Oops, I didn't mean to _____. Sorry about that!

9. Excuse me, I didn't mean to interrupt you. Please keep going.

10. I regret the way I acted during _____. Please forgive me.

 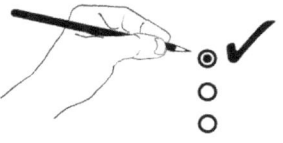

Chapter Review

It is human nature to become defensive when feeling criticized. Even though this is a natural response, it tends to perpetuate the argument and escalate the attack-defend cycle. You can de-escalate a dialogue by finding the kernel of truth in the feedback and acknowledging your contribution to the problem.

Chapter Challenge

Take a picture of the 10 Ways to Say Sorry Template, and make a goal to use one of these conversation starters before the end of the day tomorrow.

Now you know how to turn an attack-defend cycle into a linear, productive conversation, but in real-life conflicts, these skills will sometimes go out the window. When conflict escalates you are at risk of doing and saying things you might regret. This is why couples therapists recommend that all couples have a time-out procedure in place. The next chapter will detail what it is and how to set it up.

"Almost everything will work again if you unplug it for a few minutes, including you."[1]

Anne Lamott

Chapter 7
How to Take a Time-Out
Disconnect to reconnect in five simple steps

Even when you follow expert advice on how to avoid conflict and improve communication skills, there still may be times when your conversations digress. Perhaps the attack–defend cycle has escalated, or perhaps one or both of you has shut down. When this happens, it's crucial to take a break so you can return to the conversation when all parties are re-grounded and more articulate.

As arguments escalate, heart rates begin to increase and breathing becomes fast and shallow. Couples often feel trapped, and they may experience an internal state of fight-flight-or-freeze. When humans are overwhelmed with emotion, several things can happen, and none of them are helpful. When the human body gets triggered by a danger response, internal organs prepare for survival in one of the following three ways:

1. The body prepares to fight.
2. The body prepares to flee.
3. The body plays dead.

Sometimes the flight-fight-freeze reaction is obvious because tempers are flaring or someone is running out of the room. Other times it can be subtle. In the *freeze* response, a person will often shut down, go silent, and have a blank stare on their face. Let's spend some time reflecting on how this plays out with you and your partner.

Emotional Overwhelm Self-Reflection Quiz

Independent Exercise: **Partner One**

Instructions *Answer the following statements below.*

1. There have been times when our fights escalated to the point where we said or did things that we regret.

Very True   O   O   O   O   O   Very False
      1   2   3   4   5

2. Sometimes I don't even recognize myself during our arguments. I don't act the way I want to with someone I love.

Very True   O   O   O   O   O   Very False
      1   2   3   4   5

3. We stay calm and respectful and can work through our differences together even when we're triggered.

Very True   O   O   O   O   O   Very False
      1   2   3   4   5

4. When I'm emotionally overwhelmed in a disagreement I tend to want to keep talking so that we resolve the issue.

Very True   O   O   O   O   O   Very False
      1   2   3   4   5

5. We have tried taking a time-out during bad fights and it didn't work.

Very True   O   O   O   O   O   Very False
      1   2   3   4   5

6. Sometimes I get so overwhelmed that I run out of the room or hang up the phone. I feel like I can't get far enough away from the conversation.

Very True   O   O   O   O   O   Very False
      1   2   3   4   5

7. Sometimes I get so overwhelmed that I freeze and don't know what to do or say. I look blankly at my partner when they ask me questions which seems to make it worse.

Very True   O   O   O   O   O   Very False
      1   2   3   4   5

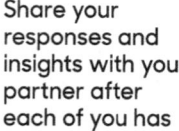

Share your responses and insights with your partner after each of you has completed your quiz.

8. We need a better way to manage when we get overwhelmed with emotion.

Very True   O   O   O   O   O   Very False
      1   2   3   4   5

Emotional Overwhelm
Self-Reflection Quiz

Independent Exercise: *Partner Two*

Instructions *Answer the following statements below.*

1. There have been times when our fights escalated to the point where we said or did things that we regret.

Very True   O   O   O   O   O   Very False
          1   2   3   4   5

2. Sometimes I don't even recognize myself during our arguments. I don't act the way I want to with someone I love.

Very True   O   O   O   O   O   Very False
          1   2   3   4   5

3. We stay calm and respectful and can work through our differences together even when we're triggered.

Very True   O   O   O   O   O   Very False
          1   2   3   4   5

4. When I'm emotionally overwhelmed in a disagreement I tend to want to keep talking so that we resolve the issue.

Very True   O   O   O   O   O   Very False
          1   2   3   4   5

5. We have tried taking a time-out during bad fights and it didn't work.

Very True   O   O   O   O   O   Very False
          1   2   3   4   5

6. Sometimes I get so overwhelmed that I run out of the room or hang up the phone. I feel like I can't get far enough away from the conversation.

Very True   O   O   O   O   O   Very False
          1   2   3   4   5

7. Sometimes I get so overwhelmed that I freeze and don't know what to do or say. I look blankly at my partner when they ask me questions which seems to make it worse.

Very True   O   O   O   O   O   Very False
          1   2   3   4   5

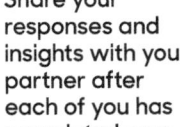

Share your responses and insights with your partner after each of you has completed your quiz.

8. We need a better way to manage when we get overwhelmed with emotion.

Very True   O   O   O   O   O   Very False
          1   2   3   4   5

What to Do When Someone Becomes Emotionally Overwhelmed

If one or both of you begin to feel triggered or frozen during a dialogue, it is a huge mistake to try to keep talking. It's impossible to have a productive conversation if you're in an acute state of physiological arousal, and you might find yourself saying and doing things you regret.

It's challenging to take a time-out during a conflict. Usually, one person desperately wants some room to breathe and the other, equally desperately, wants to keep talking.

Both partners want peace, but they may see a different avenue to find it. One is looking for reassurance through connection, and the other is looking for peace through silence or physical separation. The solution is to allow **both** to occur: Take a break *now* and return to the conversation *later*.

How to Take a Time-Out

The goal is to devise a self-care plan in advance so that you have it handy at the first warning signs that a conversation is escalating. The sooner one or both of you follow your self-care plan, the easier it will be. It can be hard to disengage from a fight, especially if taking a break in the past hasn't worked. The two most common reasons time-out procedures fail are either: (1) the request wasn't honored and someone kept talking, or (2) you never returned to the topic after the break.

For a time-out to work, the following things must happen:

- A temporary physical separation must occur

- Both parties work on self-soothing during their time apart

- The couple returns after the break to decide what to do next

Creating Your Own Time-Out Procedure

Here is an overview of the steps to creating your personalized time-out procedure.

1. Notice symptoms of fight, flight, or freeze

2. Ask for a time-out

3. Set a 20-minute timer

4. Self-soothe during your 20-minute break

5. Reconnect and agree on what to do next <- Don't skip this step!

The following section will walk you through each step.

5 Steps to Take a Time-Out

Step 1
Notice Symptoms of Fight, Flight, or Freeze

Respond to the smoke; don't wait for the fire. It's good to get in the habit of noticing what's happening in your body during a tense conversation. Pay attention to a rising heart rate, racing thoughts, holding your breath, and muscle tension.

Step 2
Ask for a Time-out

Honor the warning signs and ask for a time-out as soon as you notice the red flags. Resist the urge to explain why you are calling a time-out, and make a short and clear request. Here are some examples

- Make a "T" signal with your hands.
- Say, "Let's follow our time-out plan."
- Say, "I'm triggered and calling a time-out."

Resist the urge to explain why you are calling a time-out.

Step 3
Set a 20-Minute Timer That Both of You Can Hear

Choose what works for you: Alexa, an old-fashioned egg timer, the microwave, or a cell-phone alert. The time-out should be ***at least 20 minutes long, but not more than 2 hours.***

Step 4
Self-Soothe during Your 20-Minute Break

Use your time to take care of yourself and allow your body to relax. Actively redirect your energy away from the content of the argument so that you avoid obsessing about how you are right and your partner is wrong. Instead, engage in a distraction activity that you enjoy like taking a shower, listening to your favorite music or taking a brisk walk. Avoid driving a vehicle or operating machinery at this time.

Step 5
Reconnect and Agree on What to Do Next

Once your timer goes off, it's time to touch base with your partner. You might not be ready to talk about the original topic, and that's fine. You don't need to talk about it right away, but what you ***do*** need is to commit to a time to continue the dialogue. "Let's talk about this later" is not good enough. It should be something like, "Let's talk about this tomorrow morning over breakfast."

When it's time to resume the conversation, review the Gentle Startup formula from Chapter 5 to begin the dialogue in a positive, goal-directed manner. To set yourselves up for success, choose a time when you generally feel well-rested, grounded, and free from distractions.

Time-Out Cheat Sheet

What Are Your Red Flags?

Heart racing

Holding your breath, or taking light, irregular breaths

Light-headedness

Not listening as well as you normally do

Getting confused and disoriented

Having trouble finding words

Voice tone gets louder and edgier

Voice tone gets quiet and monotone

Overcome by defensiveness and self-righteousness

Overcome by a desire to "win the fight"

Overwhelmed with multiple emotions

Mind goes blank

Mind starts racing

Feeling like nothing is safe to say out loud

Sudden feeling of physical exhaustion

Feeling frozen, like "a deer in headlights"

Clenching your fists

Constricting your facial muscles, especially your jaw and/or brow

Feeling like you're going to vomit

Strong impulse to run out of the room or hang up the phone

Strong impulse to say or do hurtful things

Strong urgency not to let your partner leave

Urgent attempts to up the ante, such as threats of separation

How to Use Your 20-Minute Break

What *To* Do

Go for a 20-minute walk

Go for a 20-minute run

Take a showaer

Do yoga

Listen to music

Write in a journal

Do a crafts project or jigsaw puzzle

Read

Meditate

Pray

Stretch

Play a video game

Do a chore you find satisfying

Watch a funny video

Play with your pet

Lift weights or do 20 minutes of cardio

Do some gardening

What *Not* To Do

Count all the ways you are right and your partner is wrong

Think about what you're going to say when the time-out is over

Replay the conversation over and over in your head

Fantasize about leaving

Fantasize about how life would be better with someone else

Plan how to show your partner how bad it feels

Call a friend or family member to talk to someone "on your side"

Get behind the wheel of a vehicle

Drink alcohol

Take recreational drugs

Binge eat

Physically harm yourself

Involve your children in the conflict in any way

"Taking a break is not a sign of weakness. It's an act of self-care that allows you to come back stronger and more focused than ever."[2]

Lalah Delia

Identify Your Strengths and Challenges

Independent Exercise: **Partner One**

Instructions *Answer the questions below.*

1. Refer to the "What Are Your Red Flags?" list on the previous page to identify your 3 most common symptoms of emotional overwhelm.

1. ....

2. ....

3. ....

2. Choose your 3 favorite strategies from the What To Do column of of the Time-Out Cheat Sheet

1. ....

2. ....

3. ....

3. Choose your 3 most challenging counterproductive activities from the What **Not** to Do column of the Time-Out Cheat Sheet

1. ....

2. ....

3. ....

Identify Your Strengths and Challenges
Independent Exercise: *Partner Two*

Instructions *Answer the questions below.*

1. Refer to the "What Are Your Red Flags?" list on the previous page to identify your 3 most common symptoms of emotional overwhelm.

1.
....

2.
....

3.
....

2. Choose your 3 favorite strategies from the What To Do column of of the Time-Out Cheat Sheet

1.
....

2.
....

3.
....

3. Choose your 3 most challenging counterproductive activities from the What **Not** to Do column of the Time-Out Cheat Sheet

1.
....

2.
....

3.
....

Set Up Your Personal Time-Out Procedure

Joint Exercise

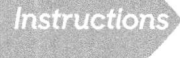

Instructions ▶ *Collaborate to devise your Joint Time-Out Procedure by discussing the following topics together*

1. Decide how you're going to ask for a time-out in a short, direct way. Here are some examples

   - Make a "T" signal with your hands

   - Say, "Let's follow our time-out plan now."

   - Choose a code word

2. Decide what kind of timer you're going to use (ie each set up on our phones or use a timer both can hear)

3. Make a verbal commitment to each other to follow these guidelines

   - Honor your partner's request for a time-out, no questions asked.

   - Return to your partner after 20 minutes. If either one of you is still not ready to address the issue at that time, schedule a concrete time and place to continue the conversation.

   - Honor the scheduled conversation even if it feels like you don't need to.

   - Treat each other with warmth and compassion in the time preceding your scheduled conversation.

3. Take turns sharing your responses from the "Identify Your Strengths and Challenges" independent exercise.

4. Make a verbal commitment to each other to follow these guidelines after your return from your 20-Minute Break:

 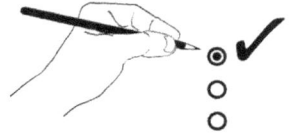

Chapter Review

Emotional overwhelm causes the body to go into a fight, flight, or freeze response which makes productive dialogue impossible. The best way to avoid unnecessary pain is to take a break when one or both people feel triggered. This plan should be set up in advance, similar to a fire-safety plan, so that both parties know the drill.
Here is a review of the five steps:

Step 1: Notice your red flags

Step 2: Ask for a time out

Step 3: Set a 20-minute timer that you both can hear

Step 4: Self-soothe during your 20-minute time-out

Step 5: Re-connect and agree on what to do next

Chapter Challenge

Flip back through this chapter and take a picture, or photocopy, the lists and cheatsheets you want to have for quick reference.

This concludes our conflict management section.
Next, we'll move into empathy training.

"If we can share our story with someone who responds with empathy and understanding, shame can't survive."[1]

Brené Brown

Chapter 8
How to Empathize
So that you both feel understood

It's lonely and frustrating to be misunderstood and calming to receive the reassurance of a listening ear from someone who cares. We feel valued when someone is willing to sit down next to us in our pain; not trying to fix it, or convince us it's not that bad, just to listen. This skill, called empathy, is how to show your partner you care.

Couples sometimes fall short on providing empathy for each other even when there is deep respect, concern, and love. Empathy is intuitive for many people, but not for everyone. Some people can't bear to watch the news; they empathize deeply with every story of suffering as if it was their own. Others see the world through a more logical lens and can more easily compartmentalize their emotions. It's helpful to know where each of you falls on this continuum.

Emotion Versus Logic Self-Reflection

Independent Exercise: **Partner One**

 **Instructions** ⟩ *Answer the questions below to reflect on your feelings about feelings.*

1. How would you describe yourself?

   A. I make decisions with my heart and am very in touch with how I feel.
   B. I make decisions through logic and by analyzing a situation.
   C. I make decisions with both logic and intuition depending on the situation.
   D. Something else:

2. How do you feel when people talk to you about their emotions?

   A. I like it. Hearing how someone feels helps me feel closer to them.
   B. I feel honored that they're talking to me, but I am worried I'll say the wrong thing.
   C. I feel the strong impulse to offer relief by fixing the problem..
   D. Something else:

3. How do you feel about sharing your strong emotions with others?

   A. I am an open book and like to share my emotions freely.
   B. It's hard for me to talk about my emotions but I see the value in it and am working to share more with people I trust.
   C. I don't see the value in talking about my emotions. They cause drama which I like to avoid.
   D. Something else:

4. How much did people talk about emotions growing up in your family?

   A. We talked about our feelings regularly.
   B. We sometimes talked about our feelings when a major event occurred.
   C. We hardly ever talked about our feelings.
   D. Something else:

Share your responses and insights with your partner after each of you has completed your quiz.

5. How do you feel about improving your empathy skills?

   A. I'm a great empathizer already and don't think I need to practice (my time would be better spent elsewhere).
   B. I think empathy is an important skill and I'd like to keep working to get better and better at it.
   C. I am skeptical about the value of improving empathy.
   D. Something else:

Emotion Versus Logic
Self-Reflection
Independent Exercise: **Partner Two**

Instructions *Answer the questions below to reflect on your feelings about feelings.*

1. How would you describe yourself?

   A. I make decisions with my heart and am very in touch with how I feel.
   B. I make decisions through logic and by analyzing a situation.
   C. I make decisions with both logic and intuition depending on the situation.
   D. Something else:

2. How do you feel when people talk to you about their emotions?

   A. I like it. Hearing how someone feels helps me feel closer to them.
   B. I feel honored that they're talking to me, but I am worried I'll say the wrong thing.
   C. I feel the strong impulse to offer relief by fixing the problem..
   D. Something else:

3. How do you feel about sharing your strong emotions with others?

   A. I am an open book and like to share my emotions freely.
   B. It's hard for me to talk about my emotions but I see the value in it and am working to share more with people I trust.
   C. I don't see the value in talking about my emotions. They cause drama which I like to avoid.
   D. Something else:

4. How much did people talk about emotions growing up in your family?

   A. We talked about our feelings regularly.
   B. We sometimes talked about our feelings when a major event occurred.
   C. We hardly ever talked about our feelings.
   D. Something else:

Share your responses and insights with your partner after each of you has completed your quiz.

5. How do you feel about improving your empathy skills?

   A. I'm a great empathizer already and don't think I need to practice (my time would be better spent elsewhere).
   B. I think empathy is an important skill and I'd like to keep working to get better and better at it.
   C. I am skeptical about the value of improving empathy.
   D. Something else:

How to Empathize Step-by-Step

The remainder of this chapter will detail the step-by-step process of what to say to each other when one of you is upset.

Almost all couples therapy techniques offer their clients at least one intervention to help them feel more understood in their conversations about painful events. Different theoretical frameworks provide different styles of empathy training but tend to have one thing in common: the speaker starts a conversation and the listener reflects back on what they heard before deepening the dialogue. This type of process is known by many names, including mirroring, active listening, reflective listening, non-violent communication, the Gottman-Rapoport intervention, and Dancing the EFT Tango.

    If you were in a couples therapist's office, your clinician would guide you along in a speaker/listener conversation to help you practice empathy. This couples therapy workbook can serve as a stand-in tool, with boxes and arrows guiding you in lieu of a live practitioner. By following the Ultimate Empathy Flowchart depicted on the next page, you can practice this exercise on your own. It is a visual representation of the decision-making tree therapists teach their clients as they coach them to support each other during times of stress or upset. The remainder of this chapter will walk you through the process of how to empathize step by step.

Citing the sources for all the strategies that have informed the empathy training flowchart is difficult since many of these terms are so widely used and it is hard to pinpoint who used them first. Additionally, over a long career and having had the privilege of learning from so many inspiring teachers and mentors, I have inevitably forgotten some names and methods from the list below, despite my best efforts. As well as acknowledgment, this list may provide some inspiration for further reading, if you are so inclined.

"Mirroring" is a term used in Imago Relationship Therapy, a framework developed by Dr. Harville Hendrix and Dr. Helen LaKelly Hunt in 1980 and described in Hendrix's book *Getting The Love You Want: A Guide for Couples* (1988). I am unaware of a particular origin or source for "active listening" and "reflective listening" but information on both is widely available online. Marshall Rosenberg outlines his "non-violent communication" techniques in his acclaimed book *Nonviolent Communication: A Language of Life* (1999). I learned about the "Gottman-Rapoport Institute"" through my Level 2 Clinical Training with Gottman Method. And finally, the evocatively named "Dancing the EFT Tango" is described by Sue Johnson in her recent book *Attachment Theory in Practice: Emotionally Focused Therapy (EFT) with Individuals, Couples, and Families* (2019).

The Ultimate Empathy Flowchart

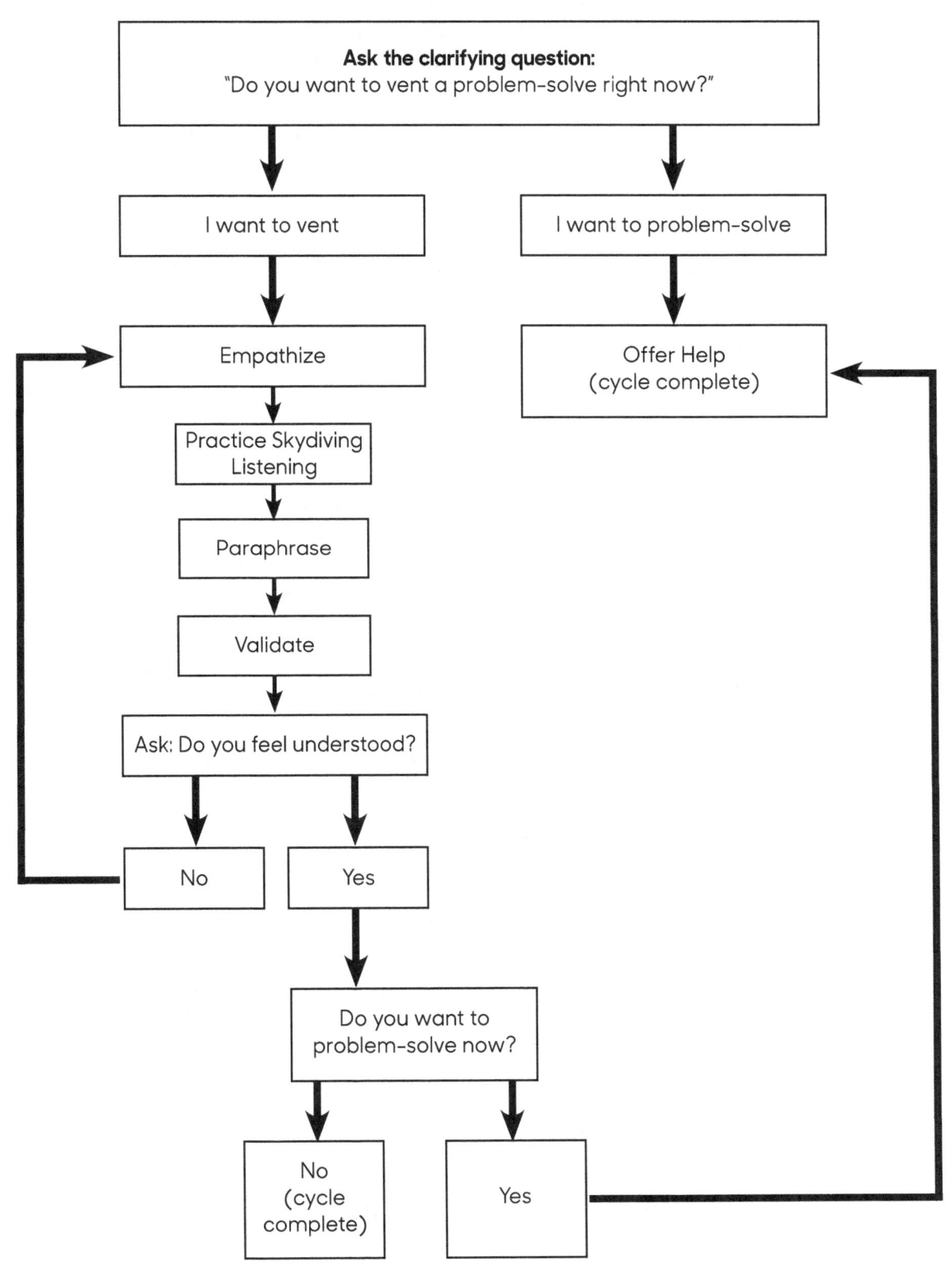

Ask the clarifying question:
"Do you want to vent a problem-solve right now?"

I want to vent

I want to problem-solve

Empathize

Offer Help
(cycle complete)

Practice Skydiving Listening

Paraphrase

Validate

Ask: Do you feel understood?

No

Yes

Do you want to problem-solve now?

No
(cycle complete)

Yes

Start at the Top of The Flowchart

It's important to make sure empathy is the right approach for the situation at hand. Active listening is not the solution to all problems. Sometimes your partner will want to talk about their feelings, and other times they might prefer concrete problem-solving, practical help, or a hug.

To make sure empathy is the right approach, you'll need to clarify the goal by following these three steps:

1. Ask the clarifying question: Do you want to vent right now or do you want help problem-solving?

2. If the answer is "I want to vent," proceed with empathy.

3. If the answer is, "I want to problem-solve," proceed with problem-solving.

If they want to vent, you'll be a neutral listening ear; if they want help, you'll share your ideas and suggestions.

Here is an example of what happens when you forget to ask the clarifying question:

Jamie: What's the matter, hon? You seem stressed.

Carson: OMG, I've got so much going on right now, I can hardly think straight. I've been awake since 5 a.m. working on this project and I still hate it, and I need to go grocery shopping because we're completely out of coffee. Plus I have a splitting headache.

Jamie: Have you drunk enough water today? I know that sometimes gives you a headache.

[Carson feels dismissed and criticized by this question and Jamie, just trying to help, doesn't understand why Carson is annoyed]

In this example, Jamie didn't like seeing Carson upset and wanted to help, but failed to ask the clarifying question. Here is how this error can be avoided:

Carson: OMG, I've got so much going on right now, I can hardly think straight. I've been awake since 5 a.m. working on this project and I still hate it, and I need to go grocery shopping because we're completely out of coffee. Plus I have a splitting headache.

Jamie: Sounds like it's been a horrible day. Do you want to talk through it or take care of your headache first?

[Carson feels validated and cared for since Jamie is giving Carson an invitation to decide what will be most helpful]

How to Empathize Step-By-Step

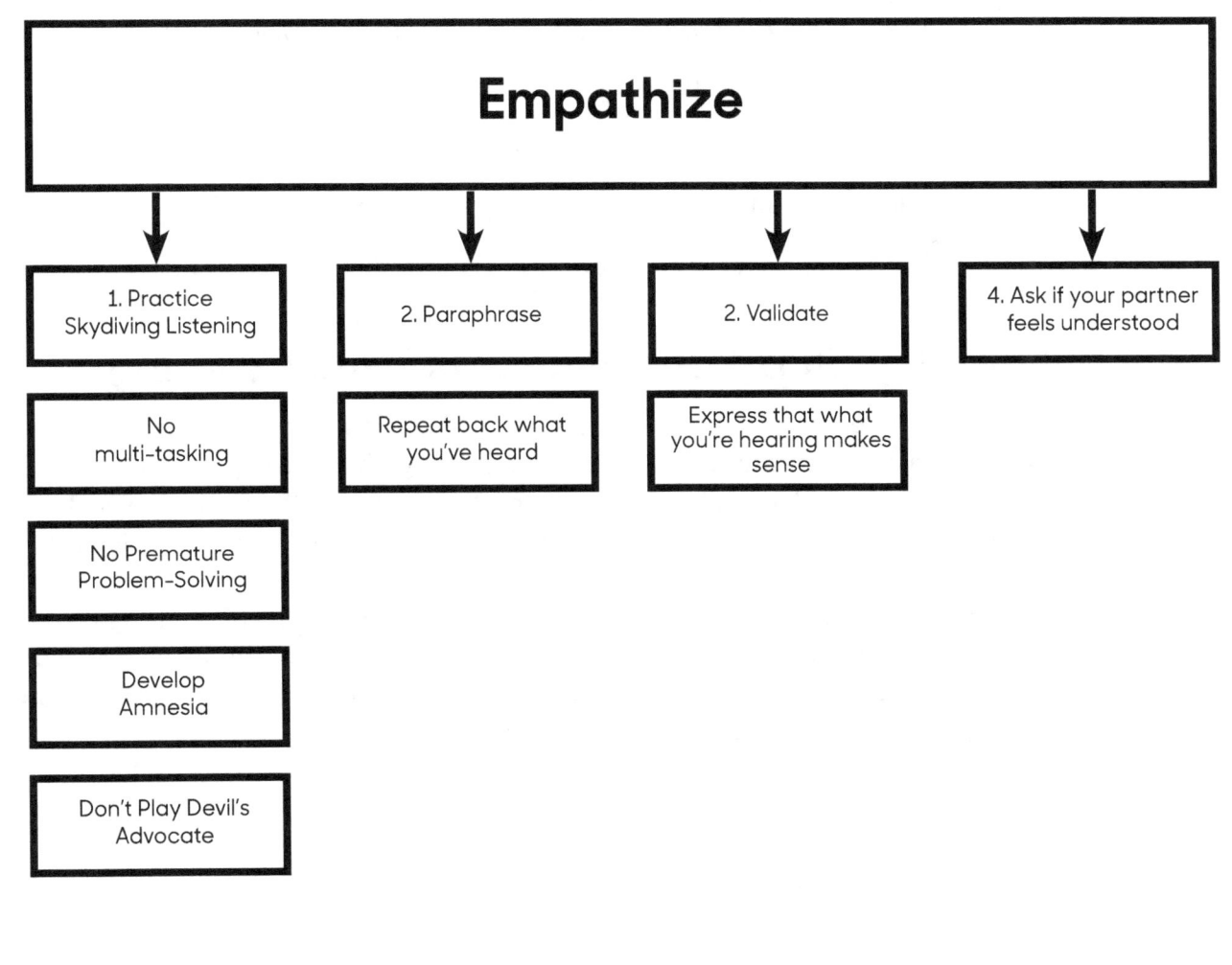

Empathize

1. Practice Skydiving Listening	2. Paraphrase	2. Validate	4. Ask if your partner feels understood
No multi-tasking	Repeat back what you've heard	Express that what you're hearing makes sense	
No Premature Problem-Solving			
Develop Amnesia			
Don't Play Devil's Advocate			

The 4 Steps of Empathy

After your partner responded to your clarifying question by mentioning they want listening not problem-solving, it's time to empathize. There are four steps to help someone feel understood when they are experiencing strong emotions and, for best results, the steps should be taken in the following sequence:

1. Practice skydiving listening.

2. Paraphrase what you hear your partner say.

3. Validate why it makes sense that your partner feels the way they do.

4. Ask them if they feel understood.

Empathy Step 1: Practice Skydiving Listening

Imagine how closely you'd be listening to your skydiving instructor right before you jumped out of a plane. Every ounce of your being would be hyper-focused on making sure you understood the instructions. You'd ask for clarification if you didn't understand something, listen closely to everything they said, and take special notice of the things they are emphasizing.

Now change gears and imagine what you would **not** be doing while getting your skydiving instructions. You wouldn't be checking your phone or thinking about what you're going to do once you land. You wouldn't correct your instructor or offer your own skydiving suggestions from something you had read online.

There are four elements of skydiving listening:

1. No multitasking

2. No Premature Problem-Solving

3. Develop Amnesia

4. Don't Play Devil's Advocate

Skydiving Listening Rule #1: No Multitasking
We often describe people as either "good listeners" or "not good listeners." In truth, everyone can be a good listener, especially in a life-or-death situation. Some people think they are bad at empathy when they are just doing a little too much multitasking.

Skydiving Listening Rule #2: No Premature Problem-Solving
The second mistake people make when it comes to empathy is that they get sucked into problem-solving even when they're trying not to. When you see your partner in pain, it's human nature to want to soothe that pain by offering solutions. Resist the urge to share your own input; listen to understand, not respond.

Skydiving Listening Rule #3: Develop Amnesia

Don't forget to forget. A good empathizer is a student, not a teacher. By developing amnesia, you will be able to listen to your partner as if you've never heard their story before. It might be tempting to talk about a time you were in a similar situation in an attempt to let them know they aren't alone, but this can backfire since it changes the dialogue to be about you instead of your partner. Instead, try to bite your tongue, and forget there is a world outside of this conversation. Here are all the things you'll need to forget.

- Forget anything you already know, or think you know, about the situation.

- Forget what your partner has already told you about this topic.

- Forget that there is a world outside of this conversation.

Skydiving Listening Rule #4: Don't Play Devil's Advocate

As you listen to your partner, you might begin to see someone else's point of view in the story. However, if your partner is stressed, angry, or frustrated, this attempt to play devil's advocate will land as if you're siding with the enemy. It is unlikely to land as comfort or support.

Skydiving Listening Cheat Sheet

1. No Multitasking

2. No Premature Problem-Solving

3. Develop Amnesia

4. Don't Play Devil's Advocate

Examples of Carson Breaking The Skydiving Listening Rules

Example of multitasking

Jamie: Half my company was just laid off and I think I'm next.

Carson: *[continuing to put away groceries while talking] Oh no, that's scary.*

Example of premature problem-solving

Jamie: Half my company was just laid off and I think I'm next.

Carson: You need to call your boss right away and offer to help her with that project she's working on. Make yourself indispensable.

Example of forgetting to have amnesia

Jamie: Half my company was just laid off and I think I'm next.

Carson: I know what you're going through because I got laid off last year.

Example of playing devil's advocate

Jamie: Half my company was just laid off and I think I'm next.

Carson: I know that sucks, but sometimes companies need to downsize just to protect their bottom line. If you do get laid off, it's nothing personal.

Example of Carson using Skydiving Listening

Jamie: Half my company was just laid off and I think I'm next.

Carson: *[Puts down groceries and sits down at kitchen table across from Jamie]* Oh my gosh, Jamie, wow. Tell me what happened.

[As Jamie tells the story, Carson responds by asking for more details, and showing verbal and non-verbal support]

Skydiving Listening Practice Worksheet

Joint Exercise

Instructions

Work together to read the dialogue examples below and identify which mistake Carson or Jamie is making in their attempts to practice skydiving listening. (See the back of the book for an Answer Key.)

1. Jamie: "I'm not sure I can pay rent this month, my account is dangerously close to being overdrawn."

Carson: [Not looking up while working on a laptop] "Yeah that's annoying."

    A. Multitasking   C. Not developing amnesia

    B. Premature problem-solving   D. Playing devil's advocate

2. Jamie: "I just burned the béchamel sauce I was making for our dinner party."

Carson: ""It's fine, I'll run out to the store and buy a jar."

    A. Multitasking   C. Not developing amnesia

    B. Premature problem-solving   D. Playing devil's advocate

3. [Carson and Jamie are late for a wedding. Carson is driving and looking very frustrated by the traffic and careless drivers on the highway.]

Carson: [Half out loud, half to self] "These drivers are crazy. No one is going to get anywhere any faster by honking their horn!"

Jamie: "They're just as frustrated as we are, everyone hates being stuck in traffic."

    A. Multitasking   C. Not developing amnesia

    B. Premature problem-solving   D. Playing devil's advocate

4. Carson: "I promised myself I was going to start exercising, yet the entire week went by and I didn't even take a walk."

Jamie: "Yes, you did. Remember we walked to the library yesterday."

    A. Multitasking   C. Not developing amnesia

    B. Premature problem-solving   D. Playing devil's advocate

5. Carson: "I saw on the news that there was another shooting in my mom's neighborhood."

Jamie: "Tell her to come live with us. She deserves to feel safe in her home."

    A. Multitasking   C. Not developing amnesia

    B. Premature problem-solving   D. Playing devil's advocate

6. Jamie: "I'm not sure I can pay rent this month, my account is dangerously close to being overdrawn."

Carson: "I know that's frustrating and scary, but you have to admit, your landlord has given you a break so many times. Eventually she's going to get fed up with this pattern, you can't blame her".

    A. Multitasking   C. Not developing amnesia

    B. Premature problem-solving   D. Playing devil's advocate

Empathy Step 2: Paraphrase

Now that you've successfully given your partner your undivided attention with skydiving listening, the second step in the process of empathy is to paraphrase what you heard with compassion until your partner feels understood.

Start by repeating back what they said to you by starting your sentence, "What I hear you saying is..." Most people feel comforted and connected when they hear their words repeated back. It will only land as "dumbing down" if your words are void of tender compassion.

The art of paraphrasing requires the ability to choose your own words while maintaining the integrity of the other person's message. This is not about whether you agree or disagree, it's about whether you **heard and understood** the core message.

Empathy Step 3: Validate

After paraphrasing what was shared with you, the third step in the empathy process is to validate the emotions. Let them know their feelings make sense to you.

Validating can sometimes be difficult because you might **not** feel that what your partner is saying makes sense. You might think they are overreacting, or focusing on the wrong part of the experience. It can be very hard to remember the amnesia rule during this phase in the process. Focus on your partner's *emotions* instead of facts because no one can ever be wrong about how they feel. Remind yourself that you can bring up your thoughts and insights at a later time after completing the empathy flowchart.

Empathy Step 4: Ask Your Partner If They Feel Understood

After you finish paraphrasing and validating, it's important to check in with your partner to see if you're getting it right and that they are beginning to feel better. Here are some ideas for how you can phrase the question.

- Am I getting it right?

- Did I miss anything?

- Do you feel understood?

- Is there anything else you want to tell me?

- Keep going if it's helping to talk it out. I'm listening.

If your partner indicates that they do not feel understood, keep empathizing. If your partner feels understood, ask them if they now want to problem-solve and proceed accordingly.

Validation Practice Worksheet
Joint Exercise

Instructions *Work together to read the examples below and circle the best examples of validation (assuming an accurate paraphrase has already occurred). Check your work in the answer key.*

1. "It makes sense to me that you're feeling mentally and physically exhausted right now. You've been burning the candle at both ends and have hardly gotten any sleep."

2. "Let's get this over with right now. Pick up the phone and call your brother."

3. "It doesn't help to just sit around and let fear control your life."

4. "Oh, babe. It seems like you're really beating yourself up over this."

5. "I see how tired you are all the time. You're working so hard that you fall asleep even during our favorite show which isn't like you."

6. "Did you know that sleep deprivation is one of the methods they use to torture prisoners? It's not healthy to be working so hard."

7. "I know how much you worry about your mom, and it's especially difficult because she values her independence so much. You don't want to take that away from her, but also want her to feel safe. It's so hard."

8. "Try not to be an angry person. My grandmother used to say you catch more flies with honey than vinegar."

Empathy Self-Reflection
Independent Exercise: *Partner One*

Instructions — *Read the statements below and indicate whether you agree or disagree.*

1. Avoiding multi-tasking is a strength for me. When my partner is feeling a strong emotion I generally put aside what I'm doing and give them my undivided attention.

Strongly Agree ○ 1 ○ 2 ○ 3 ○ 4 ○ 5 *Strongly Disagree*

2. Premature problem-solving is an area I'd like to improve. Sometimes I jump in with solutions when my partner just wants me to listen.

Strongly Agree ○ 1 ○ 2 ○ 3 ○ 4 ○ 5 *Strongly Disagree*

3. I play devil's advocate a lot. I'm the kind of person who can see everyone's point of view, so sometimes it can seem like I'm "siding with the enemy."

Strongly Agree ○ 1 ○ 2 ○ 3 ○ 4 ○ 5 *Strongly Disagree*

4. I don't like paraphrasing what someone else is saying because I'm not sure how to do it without sounding insincere.

Strongly Agree ○ 1 ○ 2 ○ 3 ○ 4 ○ 5 *Strongly Disagree*

5. I'm pretty good at validating my partner's perspective even when it differs from my own.

Strongly Agree ○ 1 ○ 2 ○ 3 ○ 4 ○ 5 *Strongly Disagree*

6. It is a strength of mine to communicate compassion with my facial expressions, body language, and voice tone.

Strongly Agree ○ 1 ○ 2 ○ 3 ○ 4 ○ 5 *Strongly Disagree*

7. I agree that empathy is an important part of relationship health and I am willing to work to improve this skill.

Strongly Agree ○ 1 ○ 2 ○ 3 ○ 4 ○ 5 *Strongly Disagree*

Share your responses and insights with your partner after each of you has completed your quiz.

8. I think both of us will be happier if we learn how to follow the Empathy Flowchart.

Strongly Agree ○ 1 ○ 2 ○ 3 ○ 4 ○ 5 *Strongly Disagree*

Empathy Self-Reflection
Independent Exercise: *Partner Two*

Read the statements below and indicate whether you agree or disagree.

1. Avoiding multi-tasking is a strength for me. When my partner is feeling a strong emotion I generally put aside what I'm doing and give them my undivided attention.

Strongly Agree   O   O   O   O   O   Strongly Disagree
      1   2   3   4   5

2. Premature problem-solving is an area I'd like to improve. Sometimes I jump in with solutions when my partner just wants me to listen.

Strongly Agree   O   O   O   O   O   Strongly Disagree
      1   2   3   4   5

3. I play devil's advocate a lot. I'm the kind of person who can see everyone's point of view, so sometimes it can seem like I'm "siding with the enemy."

Strongly Agree   O   O   O   O   O   Strongly Disagree
      1   2   3   4   5

4. I don't like paraphrasing what someone else is saying because I'm not sure how to do it without sounding insincere.

Strongly Agree   O   O   O   O   O   Strongly Disagree
      1   2   3   4   5

5. I'm pretty good at validating my partner's perspective even when it differs from my own.

Strongly Agree   O   O   O   O   O   Strongly Disagree
      1   2   3   4   5

6. It is a strength of mine to communicate compassion with my facial expressions, body language, and voice tone.

Strongly Agree   O   O   O   O   O   Strongly Disagree
      1   2   3   4   5

7. I agree that empathy is an important part of relationship health and I am willing to work to improve this skill.

Strongly Agree   O   O   O   O   O   Strongly Disagree
      1   2   3   4   5

Share your responses and insights with your partner after each of you has completed your quiz.

8. I think both of us will be happier if we learn how to follow the Empathy Flowchart.

Strongly Agree   O   O   O   O   O   Strongly Disagree
      1   2   3   4   5

Real-World Empathy Practice

Time to put it all together with a real-life example. This is the longest chapter in the workbook, and this exercise will take you about twenty to thirty minutes. Feel free to take a break at this point and return when you are up for it.

Joint Exercise

Instructions *Use the Empathy Flowchart to practice the skills you learned in this chapter with your partner. Take turns as the speaker and listener and follow these four steps..*

Use the Empathy Flowchart to practice the skills you learn in this chapter with your partner. Here is a review of the steps you'll be following together:

1. The speaker chooses an external topic to discuss. Examples: work-related stress, conflict with a friend, personal fears or insecurities, health challenges, etc.

2. The listener asks the clarifying question

3. The speaker indicates they want emotional support rather than problem-solving

4. Proceed through the Ultimate Empathy Flowchart step-by-step [See page [?], using the 4 Steps of Empathy [See pages 107 and 109].

Tips for Success

- When it is your turn to be the speaker, you are free to talk in as much detail as you like.

- Gently redirect the conversation if it starts to shift away from the original topic.

- Allow yourself to let loose and share your feelings, remembering that your partner is there to listen.

- When it is your turn to be the listener, follow the four rules of skydiving listening. If your partner gets stuck, here are some questions and prompts to encourage them to keep going.

    - Tell me what happened.

    - How have you been feeling about this?

    - Are you worried about what might happen next?

    - I'd love to hear more.

    - Were you triggered by something specific?

    - Begin paraphrasing and validating as your partner shares their experience.

 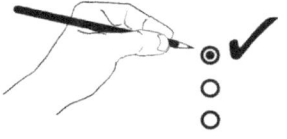

Chapter Review

Empathy is the super glue that keeps relationships bonded. When our loved ones are upset, the best thing we can do for them is to give them our undivided attention.

Keep practicing these empathy skills. It may feel phony or unnatural at first, but it's worth continuing to practice as you find and develop your own personal style. Stay in connection with your partner about whether the process is working for you both and tweak the exercises according to what works best for your specific styles and preferences.

Chapter Challenge

Try out this skill by the end of the day tomorrow. You can experiment with anyone in your life who expresses something they are upset about. Simply paraphrase what they said with an authentic, compassionate tone and see what happens.

Side by side with empathy is intimacy. Turn the page for a deep dive into how to stay physically and emotionally close.

"*You have to be strong enough to be weak.*"[1]

Jon Kabat-Zinn

Chapter 9
How to Stay Connected

Build intimacy through physical, emotional, and intellectual vulnerability

Congratulations on the work you have put in so far. You've educated yourself about how to improve communication, conflict management, and empathy skills. This chapter is about physical, emotional, and intellectual intimacy.

There is a reason the poets write about **falling** in love rather than **being** in love. Free-falling is terrifying because you don't know whether you're going to fall flat and get hurt or be caught and safely held. It feels safer to remain on solid ground.

Close connection and trust are built through a gradual process of facing your fears of rejection and hurt by sharing your vulnerability with your partner.[2] As you reassure each other that this process is safe you can slowly let go, go deeper, and feel closer. In the last chapter we worked on feeling *understood*, and this chapter will focus on feeling *loved*. We yearn to feel close and safe and together in the world. Intimacy is the result of moving from "me" to "we."

Note: A history of trauma, medical issues, or other complex variables can also impact intimacy. In these cases, I recommend seeking outside help.

Intimacy True or False Quiz
Independent Exercise: Partner One

Instructions

Answer the following true or false questions. This exercise is for self-reflection purposes only. There are no right or wrong answers.

1. I feel very close and connected to my partner, but want to feel even closer.

Very True ○ ○ ○ ○ ○ Very False
           1 2 3 4 5

2. It's very hard for me to say, "I don't know."

Very True ○ ○ ○ ○ ○ Very False
           1 2 3 4 5

3. It's hard for me to share my feelings because I don't want to get hurt.

Very True ○ ○ ○ ○ ○ Very False
           1 2 3 4 5

4. It's hard for me to initiate physical affection due to my fear of rejection.

Very True ○ ○ ○ ○ ○ Very False
           1 2 3 4 5

5. I feel emotionally connected to my partner.

Very True ○ ○ ○ ○ ○ Very False
           1 2 3 4 5

6. I feel physical intimacy is a strength for us.

Very True ○ ○ ○ ○ ○ Very False
           1 2 3 4 5

7. I have a lot to learn from my partner.

Very True ○ ○ ○ ○ ○ Very False
           1 2 3 4 5

8. I know my partner believes they have a lot to learn from me.

Very True ○ ○ ○ ○ ○ Very False
           1 2 3 4 5

9. I'd feel closer if my partner shared their feelings more.

Very True ○ ○ ○ ○ ○ Very False
           1 2 3 4 5

10. I'd feel closer if we had a more vibrant sex life.

Very True ○ ○ ○ ○ ○ Very False
           1 2 3 4 5

Share your responses and insights with your partner after each of you has completed your quiz.

Intimacy True or False Quiz
Independent Exercise: **Partner Two**

Instructions Answer the following true or false questions. This exercise is for self-reflection purposes only. There are no right or wrong answers.

1. I feel very close and connected to my partner, but want to feel even closer.

Very True   O   O   O   O   O   Very False
           1   2   3   4   5

2. It's very hard for me to say, "I don't know."

Very True   O   O   O   O   O   Very False
           1   2   3   4   5

3. It's hard for me to share my feelings because I don't want to get hurt.

Very True   O   O   O   O   O   Very False
           1   2   3   4   5

4. It's hard for me to initiate physical affection due to my fear of rejection.

Very True   O   O   O   O   O   Very False
           1   2   3   4   5

5. I feel emotionally connected to my partner.

Very True   O   O   O   O   O   Very False
           1   2   3   4   5

6. I feel physical intimacy is a strength for us.

Very True   O   O   O   O   O   Very False
           1   2   3   4   5

7. I have a lot to learn from my partner.

Very True   O   O   O   O   O   Very False
           1   2   3   4   5

8. I know my partner believes they have a lot to learn from me.

Very True   O   O   O   O   O   Very False
           1   2   3   4   5

9. I'd feel closer if my partner shared their feelings more.

Very True   O   O   O   O   O   Very False
           1   2   3   4   5

10. I'd feel closer if we had a more vibrant sex life.

Very True   O   O   O   O   O   Very False
           1   2   3   4   5

Share your responses and insights with your partner after each of you has completed your quiz.

How to Freefall Into Intimacy, Step by Step

Susan Johnson's attachment research found that intimacy results from vulnerability. There are three different ways to display vulnerability to your partner: Intellectually, emotionally, and physically. Each corner of this triad supports and influences the other. For example, strengthening physical intimacy can sometimes also strengthen emotional and intellectual intimacy. Vulnerability requires letting go and trusting that your partner will take care of you, even when you are showing your insecurities. You can read more about how Attachment Theory impact intimacy in adult relationships in Chapter 8 of Love Is an Action Verb (Silverstein 2022).

There are three roads to achieving intimacy:

1. Be intellectually vulnerable by admitting what you don't know.

2. Be emotionally vulnerable by sharing your feelings.

3. Be physically vulnerable by sharing your body in a way that feels good to you both.

Intellectual Vulnerability

Intellectual vulnerability means saying "I don't know" and meaning it. It's saying, "What do you think?" "What ideas do you have?" "I have a lot to learn from you." Building intimacy through intellectual vulnerability requires two things:

1. Admitting what you don't know

2. Assuming that your partner knows things that you don't

Here is a list of ways to express intellectual vulnerability:

- I don't know.

- I made a mistake.

- You're so much better at this than I am.

- How did you do that?

- Can you help me?

- What do you think?

Example of Jamie and Carson avoiding intellectual vulnerability

Jamie: What are you reading?

Carson: *King Lear*.

Jamie: Oh, I'm not a Shakespeare fan. I'm gonna make a cup of tea. Do you want one?

Nothing bad happened in this dialogue, but it was a missed opportunity for connection.

Example of Jamie and Carson showing intellectual vulnerability

Jamie: What are you reading?

Carson: *King Lear*.

Jamie: I tried reading Shakespeare in high school and I never really understood it. Can you explain it to me in simpler language?

Carson: Of course! The language is hard to follow, but the story is fascinating. *[Explains the plot of* King Lear *to Jamie. Jamie becomes riveted, finding Carson's excitement contagious]*

This conversation offers them a shared experience that they wouldn't have had if Jamie hadn't been open and willing to learn from Carson.

Intellectual Vulnerability Practice Worksheet
Joint Exercise

Instructions Work together to put a checkmark next to best examples of intellectual vulnerability from the list below.

1. I am really bad at remembering names. Can you remind me which of your cousins are which?

2. I'll take care of this.

3. I could really use your help with this if you have time.

4. All we have to do is come up with a plan and follow it. It's pretty simple.

5. I've been doing this for 15 years. Will you please trust me on this?

6. Can you show me how you fold shirts like that? They look so awesome in your drawer!

7. Don't worry about me, I've got this.

8. What do you think I should say to my boss?

9. Which color do you think will go best to match our dining room?

10. I know what I'm doing.

Be Intellectually Vulnerable with Each Other
Joint Exercise

Instructions Take turns using these conversation starters to practice intellectual vulnerability.

1. I really admire your ability to _____., and I'd love to learn more from you.

2. How did you get so good at _____ ?

3. Why is _____ so important to you?

4. Can you teach me how to _____ ?

5. I see how hard you have worked to learn how to _____ . What did you learn along the way?.

Emotional Vulnerability

The second corner of the triad of intimacy is emotional vulnerability. Emotional connection deepens when partners share raw feelings and authenticity. It might be tempting sometimes to be "strong" or "not burden your partner with your feelings," but in the long run, this can lead to distancing.

Similarly it is important to honor your partner's feelings when they open up to you. If you share a painful or sensitive emotion and it is ignored, it will become harder to keep sharing. Emotional closeness results when both partners build connection by sharing feelings and tenderly listening with empathy. (See Chapter 8 for more guidance on how to empathize.)

Here are some examples to get you started:

- Saying "I love you" even when your partner is getting on your nerves

- Sharing your fears of failure

- Telling your partner when you're irritated

- Being honest and specific when your partner asks you how your day was

- Allowing yourself to break down and let tears flow freely

Example of emotional guardedness

Jamie: Did you hear that the hurricane is heading in our direction? There have already been five casualties.

Carson: Yes. Good thing we have homeowner's insurance!
[Both laugh and try to pretend they are not frightened]

Example of emotional vulnerability

Jamie: Did you hear that a hurricane is heading in our direction? There have already been five casualties.

Carson: OMG. That's so sad, and I'm not gonna lie, I'm legit terrified right now!

Jamie: Me too! [They hug and then search for safely recommendations together.]

Emotional Vulnerability Practice Worksheet

Joint Exercise

Instructions → *Work together as a team to circle the responses from the list below that illustrate emotional vulnerability. (Answers are in the Appendix.)*

1. I am really embarrassed that I forgot your cousin's name.

2. I'm fine, it's just been really busy lately.

3. I miss my dad so much and can't believe he's never coming back.

4. Time heals all wounds.

5. I think I might be falling in love with you.

6. I'm trying not to dwell on this, it will only make it worse.

7. Deep down I think I'm still afraid you might leave me for someone smarter or more attractive.

8. I'm totally fine. I believe the world never gives me more than I can handle.

9. I'm freaking out about my presentation and hope I don't get up there and forget everything I know.

10. Give me a minute, I'll be right there (said from the bathroom wiping away tears).

Be Emotionally Vulnerable with Each Other

Joint Exercise

Instructions → *Be emotionally vulnerable with each other; by taking turns sharing your feelings. Use the conversation starters below to get started.*

1. Lately I've been feeling _____ about _____.

2. One of my insecurities is _____.

3. Sometimes I'm afraid that _____.

4. To be honest, I've been a little jealous about _____.

5. I really love you and don't tell you enough that _____.

Physical Vulnerability

Physical vulnerability is the closeness that occurs through physical touch. Sometimes it is a hand on a knee or a kiss on a forehead, and sometimes it is about being naked together and sharing your bodies in a way that feels good for both of you. The fear of sexual rejection can be intense, so it is important to treat each other with tenderness as you address physical vulnerability.

How to Be Physically Vulnerable with Your Partner

If you want more physical closeness in your relationship, it will require verbal and non-verbal communication. It may feel risky to talk about what you like, what you want, and check in with your partner about the pleasure they are feeling. Sometimes it's difficult to be physically vulnerable out of concern that your partner won't reciprocate, which could leave you feeling rejected or abandoned.

The first step is to take some time to think about what you like and what you want more of regarding physical closeness. Then you and your partner can talk about each of your feelings and start to take more risks initiating physical affection. It will take practice to become more confident saying "Yes, please" and "No, thank you" as you better understand both your areas of pleasure and insecurity.

Example of Jamie and Carson being physically guarded

[Jamie and Carson are in bed; Carson is reading and Jamie is watching TV. Jamie wants to make love but is nervous to initiate.]

Jamie: *[thinking]* It would be so nice to connect tonight. Should I grab a kiss? That would be nice.

[Looks over and sees Carson engrossed in a book] What if Carson isn't up for it and gets annoyed. Maybe I should just turn over and fall asleep. I'll initiate another night.

[Turns over and deliberately starts to think about something else to try to drift off to sleep. Carson, still reading, is completely clueless that any of this is going on.]

Example of Jamie and Carson being physically vulnerable

[Jamie and Carson are in bed; Carson is reading and Jamie is watching TV]

Jamie: *[thinking]* It would be so nice to connect tonight. Should I grab a kiss? That would be nice.

[Looks over and sees Carson engrossed in a book] Okay, let me just get up the courage to initiate even though Carson might not be in the mood.

[Jamie reaches over and strokes Carson's hair. Carson turns to face Jamie and is smiling. They share a tentative kiss. Jamie wants to keep going but Carson doesn't.]

Carson: *[out loud]* This feels good. I love kissing you but have to be honest, I'm pretty exhausted and am not up for much more than that tonight.

Physical Vulnerability Practice Worksheet

Joint Exercise

Instructions *Work together as a team to check the responses from the list below that illustrate physical vulnerability. (Answers are in the Appendix.)*

1. Grabbing your partner's hand during a movie.

2. Waiting for your partner to kiss you because you prefer to be pursued.

3. Asking for a hug.

4. Pretending you're asleep because you don't want to be intimate.

5. Choosing the same sofa as your partner so you can snuggle.

6. Going up to bed early hoping your partner will notice you want intimacy.

7. Kissing your partner passionately when they come home.

8. Complaining to your friends about your sex life with your partner.

9. Telling your partner what feels good to your body.

10. Asking your partner what feels good to their body.

11. Silently wishing your partner would pay more attention to your intimacy needs.

12. Talking to your partner about masturbation and fantasies.

Time to Talk About Physical Intimacy

Joint Exercise

Take turns looking through this list of questions and choosing a question to ask your partner. Then, listen to their answers with tenderness. Anyone may decline to answer a particular question at any time. Remember that you may stop this dialogue if either of you becomes triggered. If this happens, you might benefit from some self-soothing and self-reflection prior to resuming a verbal discussion.

1. Is there something I can do during our lovemaking that will help you feel more comfortable or feel more pleasure?

2. Have you been feeling satisfied with the frequency of our lovemaking lately?

3. Have you been feeling satisfied with the amount of romance in our life lately?

4. When you think back, what were some of your favorite memories of physical intimacy?

5. I love it when we _____ and I'd love to do more of that. What do you think?

6. What time of day do you prefer to make love?

7. Do you wish there were more non-sexual affection in our relationship lately?

8. It's easier for me to be physically vulnerable when I feel emotionally close. How about you?

9. It's easier for me to be emotionally vulnerable when we are physically connected. How about you?

10. I'd like to try some different things in the bedroom. Would you like to hear my ideas?

11. Are there some different things you'd like to try in the bedroom?

12. Are there any fantasies you'd like to tell me about?

13. I have some fantasies I've been embarrassed to tell you. Would you like to hear about them?

14. How would you like me to communicate if you're doing something that isn't enjoyable for me? Verbally? Non-verbally?

15. How are you feeling about our monogamy agreement?

16. Do you think body image insecurity plays a role in our sex life? How so? What do you think would help?

17. What do you think would make our sex life even better than it already is?

Decide on Next Steps

Now that the two of you have learned a little bit more about how you feel and what you want, brainstorm one next step you'd like to take toward improving physical intimacy.

Joint Exercise

Instructions · *Use the space below to write down your plan.*

....

....

....

....

....

....

....

The Heart-Body-Mind Connection – Pulling It All Together

Congratulations! You have now explored the three roads to intimacy and discussed how to be more vulnerable with each other intellectually, emotionally, and physically. Connection is never linear; it is more like a circle that expands and contracts.

As you work on taking risks, it's important to do so with patience, compassion, and grace, for both yourself and your partner. Try to remember that behavioral change happens slowly. Setbacks are expected, especially during times of stress. It's worth celebrating the small improvements so that you remain motivated and supported.

 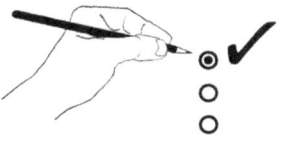

Chapter Review

The intimacy free-fall includes physical, emotional, and intellectual vulnerability. It will feel safer and safer each time you take risks and open up to one another about things that are hard to admit. Since the triad of intimacy is interconnected, sometimes working on one corner of your connection will lead to a stronger connection in another area (for example, emotional closeness can lead to physical closeness).

Chapter Challenge

Now is a good time to thank your partner again for doing this workbook with you. It is very hard to be vulnerable and share things that are hard to admit. You are lucky to have chosen a partner who is committed to relationship wellness.

Keep reading to discover how to build daily relationship habits and routines to maintain long-lasting love.

"Love at first sight is easy to understand; it's when two people have been looking at each other for a lifetime that it becomes a miracle."[1]

Amy Bloom

Chapter 10
How to Build a Relationship Routine
Invest in your partnership every single day

Most people think that the biggest risk to living happily ever after is infidelity or intense conflict. But potentially more dangerous is the invisible risk of unnoticed, gradual, steady disconnection. This happens when couples get in the habit of "going through the motions." Romantic, passionate lovers can become roommates living parallel lives, or coworkers running a household together.

The truth is that relationships rarely end due to drama or trauma.

As I've mentioned, I spend 40 hours a week helping people save their marriages. They often tell me they wish they had come to me earlier – and not because of the communication skills I taught them or learning about relational psychology. The main reason they give for kicking themselves is how easy and obvious some of the work is. Just adding tiny habits into their daily routine made an immense difference in how they felt about their relationship. We are so much in the habit of solving problems by decreasing negativity that we often forget to make things better by adding positivity.

In this next exercise you'll reflect on the current relationship routines you have, and the places where distance may be starting to form between you.

Relationship Routine
True or False Quiz

Independent Exercise: **Partner One**

Instructions *Answer the following true or false questions. This exercise is for self-reflection purposes only. There are no right or wrong answers.*

1. I sometimes feel like we are roommates or co-workers instead of lovers.

Very True ○ ○ ○ ○ ○ Very False
          1 2 3 4 5

2. We are good at reaching out to each other to connect during our busy lives.

Very True ○ ○ ○ ○ ○ Very False
          1 2 3 4 5

3. I worry that we are so busy with our daily lives that our relationship might slip to the back burner.

Very True ○ ○ ○ ○ ○ Very False
          1 2 3 4 5

4. Sometimes I feel taken for granted and it would mean a lot if my partner reached out to me more often.

Very True ○ ○ ○ ○ ○ Very False
          1 2 3 4 5

5. I love my partner deeply and don't want them to feel taken for granted.

Very True ○ ○ ○ ○ ○ Very False
          1 2 3 4 5

6. I think we'd be happier if we felt more like a team.

Very True ○ ○ ○ ○ ○ Very False
          1 2 3 4 5

7. We both work hard and deserve to feel more appreciated.

Very True ○ ○ ○ ○ ○ Very False
          1 2 3 4 5

Share your responses and insights with your partner after each of you has completed your quiz.

8. I feel committed to making a conscious effort to insert more connection rituals into our daily routine.

Very True ○ ○ ○ ○ ○ Very False
          1 2 3 4 5

Relationship Routine
True or False Quiz
Independent Exercise: **Partner Two**

Instructions *Answer the following true or false questions. This exercise is for self-reflection purposes only. There are no right or wrong answers.*

1. I sometimes feel like we are roommates or co-workers instead of lovers.

Very True ○ ○ ○ ○ ○ Very False
          1   2   3   4   5

2. We are good at reaching out to each other to connect during our busy lives.

Very True ○ ○ ○ ○ ○ Very False
          1   2   3   4   5

3. I worry that we are so busy with our daily lives that our relationship might slip to the back burner.

Very True ○ ○ ○ ○ ○ Very False
          1   2   3   4   5

4. Sometimes I feel taken for granted and it would mean a lot if my partner reached out to me more often.

Very True ○ ○ ○ ○ ○ Very False
          1   2   3   4   5

5. I love my partner deeply and don't want them to feel taken for granted.

Very True ○ ○ ○ ○ ○ Very False
          1   2   3   4   5

6. I think we'd be happier if we felt more like a team.

Very True ○ ○ ○ ○ ○ Very False
          1   2   3   4   5

7. We both work hard and deserve to feel more appreciated.

Very True ○ ○ ○ ○ ○ Very False
          1   2   3   4   5

♡

Share your responses and insights with your partner after each of you has completed your quiz.

8. I feel committed to making a conscious effort to insert more connection rituals into our daily routine.

Very True ○ ○ ○ ○ ○ Very False
          1   2   3   4   5

Prevention and Consistency in Less Than 10 Seconds (at a time)

It's not usually anyone's intention to move their partner to the back burner. A relationship routine is similar to any health routine, such as brushing your teeth or staying properly hydrated. Relationship wellness habits help couples remember not to inadvertently neglect or de-prioritize their partners. Relationship routines aren't hard; they just require commitment and consistency.

The Gottmans' research showed the importance of developing "rituals of connection." Little everyday habits lead to long-term relationship success. John Gottman uses the analogy of an emotional bank account: When partners reach out to connect in small ways it is like making a deposit or investment in the relationship. These bids for connection maintain a solid foundation of trust. The research showed that this was one of the core predictors of long-term relationship happiness.[1] It's like saving for retirement, except you're putting aside time instead of money; if you want to keep having fun 20 years from now, carve out a few more moments in your day for each other.

You might feel like you don't have enough time to add a single thing to your weekly routine. The good news is that we know from the research that we don't have to spend hours on these habits. Many of them take less than ten seconds at a time.

How to Make Daily Investments into Your Emotional Bank Account

You can start saving for retirement today.

You and your partner can decide which habits you want to add to your routine. It's best to brainstorm the easiest, most natural ways to add some small moments of connection to your current routine. Couples who have the most long-term success with this are not overly ambitious. Similar to going back to the gym for three hours after not working out for a while, you'll lose motivation if your plan is too difficult or time-consuming.

Let's use Carson and Jamie as an example.

Carson and Jamie's Relationship Routine

- 3-second wake-up greeting
- 6-second goodbye kiss
- 29-second daytime text
- 4-minute arrival connection time
- 30-minute device-free dinner
- 10-minute evening check-in
- 20-minute weekend roundup
- 3-hour monthly date night

Choose Your Relationship Routine
Independent Exercise: *Partner One*

Instructions *Read each sample relationship habit from the list below and check off the items you want to add or keep in your regular relationship routine.*

Daily Investments

☐ A kiss on the forehead first thing in the morning (3 seconds)

☐ Daily morning coffee or tea together (15 minutes)

☐ An extended hug or kiss as you say goodbye (6 seconds)

☐ Mid-morning appreciation text (29 seconds)

☐ Mid-afternoon update text (29 seconds)

☐ Brief check-in at the end of the day (4 minutes)

☐ Distraction-free dinner (at least 30 minutes)

☐ Evening check-in: What do you want to share with me about your day? (10 minutes)

☐ Goodnight snuggles (as long as you like)

When You're Not Together

☐ A good morning text from the first person to wake (3 seconds)

☐ Second person to wake texts a response (3 seconds)

☐ Mid-morning video call (3–15 minutes)

☐ Mid-afternoon update text (29 seconds)

☐ Trade end-of-the-day voice notes (2 minutes)

☐ Goodnight phone call" (10 minutes)

Weekly Investments

☐ Weekend roundup: How was your week? (20 minutes)

☐ Easy date night at home, virtual, or out (see Chapter 11 for a long list of date ideas)

☐ Shared errand (1 hour)

☐ Exercise together (1 hour or more)

Monthly Investments

☐ Monthly conversation: How are you really? (1 hour)

☐ Special monthly date night, virtual, or out (see Chapter 11 for a long list of date ideas)

Choose Your Relationship Habits
Independent Exercise: *Partner Two*

Instructions *Read each sample relationship habit from the list below and check off the items you want to add or keep in your regular relationship routine.*

Daily Investments

- ☐ A kiss on the forehead first thing in the morning (3 seconds)
- ☐ Daily morning coffee or tea together (15 minutes)
- ☐ An extended hug or kiss as you say goodbye (6 seconds)
- ☐ Mid-morning appreciation text (29 seconds)
- ☐ Mid-afternoon update text (29 seconds)
- ☐ Brief check-in at the end of the day (4 minutes)
- ☐ Distraction-free dinner (at least 30 minutes)
- ☐ Evening check-in: What do you want to share with me about your day? (10 minutes)
- ☐ Goodnight snuggles (as long as you like)

When You're Not Together

- ☐ A good morning text from the first person to wake (3 seconds)
- ☐ Second person to wake texts a response (3 seconds)
- ☐ Mid-morning video call (3–15 minutes)
- ☐ Mid-afternoon update text (29 seconds)
- ☐ Trade end-of-the-day voice notes (2 minutes)
- ☐ Goodnight phone call" (10 minutes)

Weekly Investments

- ☐ Weekend roundup: How was your week? (20 minutes)
- ☐ Easy date night at home, virtual, or out (see Chapter 11 for a long list of date ideas)
- ☐ Shared errand (1 hour)
- ☐ Exercise together (1 hour or more)

Monthly Investments

- ☐ Monthly conversation: How are you really? (1 hour)
- ☐ Special monthly date night, virtual, or out (see Chapter 11 for a long list of date ideas)

Plan Your Investment Strategy Together
Joint Exercise

Instructions *Work together to plan your relationship routine by adding the habits you both like. Follow the steps below and use the space provided to mark down your responses.*

Step 1: Take turns sharing your responses from the above exercise.

Step 2: Take note of the items you both chose.

Step 3: Write down 1–3 *new* habits to add to your regular routine.

....

....

....

Step 4: Write down 1–3 parts of your current routine that you will commit to keep doing.

....

....

....

 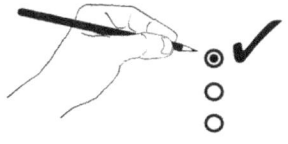

Chapter Review

The couples who find long-term happiness are the ones who regularly make time and space for each other. There is immense benefit from making small deposits into your emotional bank account on a regular basis so that you can avoid the risk of slowly drifting apart. Hugs, kisses, texts, and conversations are great ways to remind each other that you are not taken for granted.

Chapter Challenge

Hug each other right now for six whole seconds and see how it feels.

Now that you've added some prevention routines,
it's time for fun and adventure!

"The dreams that you dare to dream really do come true."[1]

Yip Harburg, lyricist of "Over the Rainbow"

Chapter 11
How to Keep Having Fun and Adventure
Don't wait for joy; go get it now

Happiness is the presence of joy, not the absence of pain. It is crucial, now and then, to stop to ponder whether or not you are enjoying your love. Are you having fun? Dreaming big dreams? Hoping for small miracles?

People sometimes take the saying "relationships are hard work" a little too seriously. They work so hard that they forget to make time for playfulness and laughter. Self-care is not a luxury; it's a necessity. And as you practice taking care of your own wants and needs, you can expand that to the concept of *relationship* care so that you can both be happier.

Making Life Dreams Come True

"Make Life Dreams Come True" is one of the foundational elements that comprise the Gottmans' "Sound Relationship House."[2] Dreams can be lofty and profound, or they can be small and sweet. It's fun to check off your bucket list items together, as well as simply enjoying a walk through a park.

Remember the reason why you're in a relationship in the first place. Maybe you still have that giddy feeling from when you first met. If so, that's awesome, but if not, no worries; it's not too late to get that feeling back if you want it.

How to Keep Having Fun and Adventure

Remembering a few guidelines can help you make sure that your relationship isn't lopsided toward too much work and not enough play.

Here are three steps you can start implementing right away.

Step 1: Increase your Vitamin N (say "no" more).
Step 2: Don't wait for fun; go get it now.
Step 3: Schedule dates and adventures.

Step 1: Increase Your Vitamin N (say "no" more)

The sheer simplicity of saying "no" a little more often can have a huge impact on relationship health. When we say "yes" to the outside world, we are inadvertently saying "no" to ourselves and our partners. We might not have that top of mind when we say "yes" to someone who is asking for a favor or volunteering for an extra project at work. Time is a limited resource and it will be swallowed up if we don't protect it, for our own happiness and to have time for the people we love most in the world. The faster pace our lives are moving, the more important it is to triage who gets our valuable time.

Vitamin N Self-Assessment True or False Quiz

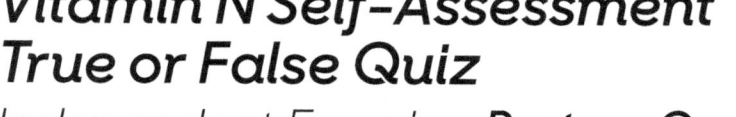

Independent Exercise: Partner One

Instructions

Answer the following true or false questions. This exercise is for self-reflection purposes only. There are no right or wrong answers.

1. I am good at saying "no" when people ask me for favors I don't want to do.

Very True   O   O   O   O   O   Very False
    1   2   3   4   5

2. I would like to improve my ability to say "no" when people ask me for favors I don't want to do.

Very True   O   O   O   O   O   Very False
    1   2   3   4   5

3. It is easier for me to offer help to others than accept help when others offer it to me.

Very True   O   O   O   O   O   Very False
    1   2   3   4   5

4. I feel an urgency to respond rapidly to emails or phone calls, even when I am having fun with my partner.

Very True   O   O   O   O   O   Very False
    1   2   3   4   5

5. I am pretty good at letting go of non-urgent tasks to prioritize the things I enjoy.

Very True   O   O   O   O   O   Very False
    1   2   3   4   5

Share your responses and insights with your partner after each of you has completed your quiz.

Vitamin N Self-Assessment
True or False Quiz

Independent Exercise: **Partner Two**

Instructions

Answer the following true or false questions. This exercise is for self-reflection purposes only. There are no right or wrong answers.

1. I am good at saying "no" when people ask me for favors I don't want to do.

Very True   O   O   O   O   O   Very False
          1   2   3   4   5

2. I would like to improve my ability to say "no" when people ask me for favors I don't want to do.

Very True   O   O   O   O   O   Very False
          1   2   3   4   5

3. It is easier for me to offer help to others than accept help when others offer it to me.

Very True   O   O   O   O   O   Very False
          1   2   3   4   5

4. I feel an urgency to respond rapidly to emails or phone calls, even when I am having fun with my partner.

Very True   O   O   O   O   O   Very False
          1   2   3   4   5

5. I am pretty good at letting go of non-urgent tasks to prioritize the things I enjoy.

Very True   O   O   O   O   O   Very False
          1   2   3   4   5

Share your responses and insights with your partner after each of you has completed your quiz.

Step 2: Don't Wait for Fun, Go Get It Now

A common mistake couples make is to postpone fun for weekends or exotic vacations. These activities can be costly, logistically difficult, or maybe even impossible. A little creativity can go a long way toward finding ways to bring amusement into otherwise dull activities.

Part of this process involves noticing your mindset. If you're stressed and irritable a lot, things aren't as funny or sweet. Tension gets in the way of pleasure, and you might try to reassure yourself by hoping that things will get better soon. But you deserve for things to get better now. This requires giving yourself a break so you can delight in yourself and delight in your relationship.

As you work to decrease stress and irritability, you can benefit from trying to insert fun into everyday life. Just as negative energy is contagious, so is playful energy. Here are some ideas to consider that might make life more playful and chores less dreadful:

- When it's time to talk about your budget, do it at your favorite brunch place.

- Be silly.

- Run errands *together* instead of dividing and conquering.

- Gently toss a snowball or pillow at your partner when they least expect it.

- Send an unexpected 😉.

Talk about Fun
Joint Exercise

Instructions *Take turns interviewing your partner by asking and answering the following questions.*

1. How do you feel about the amount of fun we have in our relationship?
2. What stands out for you as the times we have had the most fun together?
3. How do you feel about trying to choose an errand or two to do together instead of apart?
4. How are you doing when it comes to self-care/having fun on your own?
5. What can I do to support you in prioritizing the activities that you enjoy?
6. Do you think it's a good idea to try to actively initiate more play or non-sexual flirtation?

Step 3: *Schedule Dates and Adventures*

Dreams can't come true if no one is dreaming. First dates often include people talking about their life aspirations, but those kinds of conversations often become less common over time. Goals and aspirations are just as important now as when you ask a child, "What do you want to be when you grow up?"

Also, dreams can't come true if no one schedules them. Sometimes, "working on your relationship" requires things like getting a babysitter, making dinner reservations, or brainstorming fun adventures you want to have.

The remainder of this chapter is a date night planning exercise to help you make your dreams come true ...

Date Night Planner – Step 1
Choose Your Favorite
Date Ideas
Joint Exercise

Instructions *Read through the items below one at a time, and circle the items you **both** would be willing to try.*

Weekly Date Ideas

1. Watch one of your all-time favorite movies

2. Play a board game

3. Carve out time to do absolutely nothing together

4. Go for a walk

5. Go for a hike

6. Go for a run

7. Go for a bike ride

8. Play basketball

9. Play a racket sport

10. Go swimming together

11. Search YouTube for a yoga class

12. Take a drive without a destination

13. Take turns serving breakfast in bed for one another

14. Romantic dinner at home – cooking together

15. Romantic dinner at home – ordering take out

16. Write poems or love notes for one another

17. Choose a book to read together

18. Work out together

19. Go to a café

20. Go to a farmers' market

21. Go to a thrift store

22. Have a picnic in the park

23. Play a computer or video game

24. Take a bath or shower together

25. Play "Truth or Dare"

26. Play "Never Have I Ever"

27. Give one another massages

28. Make love in a new way

29. Hug or kiss for a solid 30 seconds without any expectations

30. Bake together

31. Turn out the lights and talk by candle-light

32. Share your favorite music

33. Meditate together

34. Make a scrapbook

35. Exchange greeting cards

36. Take the day off in the middle of the week to stay in together

37. Go to the mall

38. Get up early to watch the sunrise

39. Find a scenic location to watch the sunset

40. Play cards

41. Grab romantic moments during family activities

42. Run errands together

43. Have a postcard-writing party

44. Do household chores together while playing loud music

45. Take a 3-hour vacation from tech

46. Take a 12-hour vacation from tech

47. Gratitude Marathon (express 12 appreciations in 24 hours)

48. Watch your wedding video together

49. Put together a photo album

50. Join a book club

51. Go window shopping

52. Go to a bakery and impulse buy

53. Visit a farm and sample their fresh ice cream

54. Join your partner in one of their favorite hobbies

55. Road trip to a local tourist attraction you haven't visited yet

56. _____

57. _____

Monthly Date Ideas

1. Celebrate a special anniversary
2. Go out to dinner at a new restaurant
3. Go out to dinner at one of your favorite places
4. Go to the movies
5. Go to an art museum
6. Go to an arcade
7. Brunch at one of your favorite places
8. Brunch somewhere new
9. Volunteer
10. Play laser tag
11. Take an art/pottery class
12. Take a dance class
13. Take a film class
14. Take an improv class
15. Attend a poetry reading
16. Sing karaoke
17. Attend a writing workshop
18. Go horseback riding
19. Go on a double date with friends
20. Go antiquing
21. Go out for dessert
22. Go to a concert
23. Go camping
24. Go to a bed and breakfast for the weekend
25. Get a couples massage
26. Go to a spa
27. Go to an amusement park
28. Go to the beach
29. Go to a sporting event
30. Go to the opera

31. Go to the ballet

32. Go to the theater

33. Go to a comedy club

34. Go boating

35. Go to a batting cage

36. Play mini golf

37. Play golf

38. Hire a photographer for a photoshoot

39. Sign up for an athletics competition and train for it together

40. Go to a tourist event in your town

41. Go to a water park

42. Go out dancing

43. Go to a festival

44. Go to a wildlife reserve

45. Go to the zoo

46. Go to an escape room

47. Go to an aquarium

48. Go to trivia night

49. Get tattoos

50. Re-affirm your vows privately or publicly

51. Go to a drive-in movie

52. Go back to the place where you had your first kiss

53. Go to an orchard to pick your own fruits or vegetables

54. Join a local sports league (e.g. volleyball, ultimate frisbee)

55. Go to a wine tasting

56. Go to a microbrewery

57. Go to a psychic

58. Go to a local tourist attraction

59. Go to an open mic night

60. _____

61. _____

Bucket List Ideas

1. Travel to a new part of your country
2. Travel to a new continent
3. Climb a mountain
4. Go skydiving
5. Go scuba diving
6. Take a hot air balloon ride
7. Go bungee jumping
8. Return to one of your favorite vacation spots
9. Drive race-cars
10. Visit a national rainforest
11. Go to a national park
12. Go to an elephant sanctuary
13. Go to the Olympics
14. Go to the Super Bowl
15. Be in the studio audience of a TV show
16. Go to an exotic spa
17. Go to an inclusive resort
18. Go on a cruise
19. Visit one of the seven wonders of the world
20. Go on a meditation retreat
21. Get backstage passes for a concert
22. Bike across your country or region
23. Take a master class with a celebrity
24. _____
25. _____

Date Night Planner – Step 2
Narrow Down Your Top 5

Joint Exercise

 *Review your lists together and choose your five favorite ideas from each category and take notes using the space below.*

Weekly Top 5

1.
....

2.
....

3.
....

4.
....

5.
....

Monthly Top 5

1.
....

2.
....

3.
....

4.
....

5.
....

Bucket List Top 5

1.
....

2.
....

3.
....

4.
....

5.
....

Date Night Planner – Step 3
Schedule Your Fun
Joint Exercise

Instructions *Time to start scheduling by carving out some time in your calendars to make sure these dates happen. Choose one item from each category above and complete the planning exercise by filling in the blanks below:*

1. Weekly

We would both like to _____

We will do this on (date) _____ at (time) _____The following

logistics need to happen in preparation. Note who will take care of each action item.

....

....

....

2. Monthly

We would both like to _____

We will do this on (date) _____ at (time) _____The following

logistics need to happen in preparation. Note who will take care of each action item.

The following logistics need to happen in preparation. Note who will take care of each action item.

....

....

....

3. Bucket List

We would both like to _____

We will do this on (date) _____ at (time) _____The following

logistics need to happen in preparation. Note who will take care of each action item.

The following things need to happen to make this dream a reality.

....

....

....

Want to Keep Going with a Year Full of Dates?

I have created a date night planner, *52 Dates in 52 Weeks*, which includes a template for planning out an **entire year** of weekly and monthly dates. You can get your copy by going to my website: www.laurasilverstein.co. Downloading the planner will also place you on my mailing list where I share weekly relationship tips.

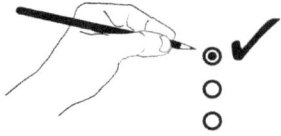

Chapter Review

You deserve to delight in your relationship. Partnerships that are defined by managing logistics and resolving conflict can lose their spark. Saying no to external requests for your time, initiating play, and scheduling date nights can keep fun and adventure in your life.

Chapter Challenge

Find an inspirational quote, song, or movie that is about believing that you can reach your dreams.

This is the last "how to" lesson of this workbook. The next chapter summarizes all of the advice in the workbook for easy reference and review.

"*The good old days are now.*"[1]

Tom Clancy

Chapter 12
Now That You Have All the Tools
Go out there and use them!

Congratulations on completing this workbook! You may be wondering, how you can possibly keep the momentum going now that you have devoted so much time to learning about relationship wellness and practicing new ways of talking to each other. You did a lot. You learned how to set your relationship goals, focus on positivity, manage conflict, and increase empathy, intimacy, and fun.

You've absorbed a great deal of information, had some important conversations, and practiced new skills. Now it's time to go out there and use these skills in the real world.

You can't unlearn what you now know, and you might find that you are applying these concepts in your everyday life without even consciously knowing that you're doing it. Now and then an "aha moment" might present itself and you and your partner will enjoy the fruits of your labor.

Here are my hopes for you as you move forward:

- You will remember you are both deeply loved.

- You will feel happier in the everyday life of your relationship.

- You have more clarity about how to deal with conflict and stress.

- You will feel more connected and understood as you practice deep listening and vulnerability.

- You will delight in your time together with daily play and long-term adventures.

Rediculously Oversimplified Review of this Workbook

1. How to set your relationship goals
Think about your relationship as a living growing system that requires work and maintenance. Then set realistic goals to be the best version of yourself.

2. How to actually be happy
Cherish the love right in front of you.

3. How to avoid a fight
Be mindful of the words you use by following Laura's 5 Communication Ground Rules.

4. How to deal with conflict
Remember that your partner will let you down, and you will let your partner down. Agree on a way to manage your differences that works for both of you.

5. How to ask for what you need
Use John Gottman's Gentle Startup formula.

6. How to respond to criticism
Find the kernel of truth in what your partner is accusing you of, and take responsibility for your contribution to the problem.

7. How to take a time-out
Notice evidence that a conversation is escalating, physically separate for 20 minutes, then come back and decide whether to keep talking or postpone the conversation.

8. How to empathize
Follow Laura's Ultimate Empathy Flowchart, forget about the world outside, and listen as if you've never heard any of this before. Avoid premature problem-solving.

9. How to stay connected
Be emotionally, physically, and intellectually vulnerable to honor your heart-mind-body connection and strengthen your intimacy.

10. How to build a relationship routine
Develop and follow a regular relationship routine to set and maintain daily habits to stay connected.

11. How to keep having fun
Say "no" more to the outside world so you can say "yes" more to your partner, integrate fun and humor into everyday life, and schedule monthly, yearly, and once-in-a-lifetime dates and adventures.

12. Start using these tools today

What Next?

You've just finished hours and hours of discussion with your partner, quizzes and self-reflection exercises. Your head might be swimming, not knowing where to start. A logical next step would be to visit my website, **www.laurasilverstein.co** where you can join my mailing list, read articles, enroll in courses, and download free printable resources.

Before you do anything else, I suggest you start by giving your partner a big hug. You'll find these concepts are all around you, and opportunities to implement this advice is everywhere.

For now, just take a break and a moment of gratitude for each other.

You guys are awesome

A Request from Laura

Please consider leaving a short review on the platform where you purchased this workbook. Just a line or two would help me get the word out.

Thank you for your support in helping me with my mission to offer affordable DIY resources as an alternative to costly couples therapy.

About Laura Silverstein, LCSW

Photo credit: Todd Zimmerman

Laura Silverstein is a recognized thought leader in the field of relationship wellness, sought out for her expert advice from media outlets such as The New York Times, Today, and Real Simple Magazine.

She is one of today's most original and insightful experts on modern relationships. Her advice is evidence-based, inclusive, jargon-free, and action-oriented. She is certified in the Gottman Method of Couples therapy and is known for helping couples focus on their strengths instead of their problems and guiding them with step-by-step action plans.

As founder and co-owner of Main Line Counseling Partners, a small private practice, in Bryn Mawr, PA, she oversees over 5,000 hours of therapy a year, manages a team of therapists, and provides workshops and training to aspiring couples therapists.

She and her family live in the suburbs of Philadelphia, which she affectionately refers to as "the city of humanly love.".

Here are some ways to contact Laura, and some options for next steps:

1. Join Laura's mailing list: go to www.laurasilverstein.co, and choose the freebie you'd like as a sign-up gift.

2. Sign up for more support: for live and online workshops visit www.laurasilverstein. co. For traditional couples therapy or private intensive sessions in the state of Pennsylvania visit www.mainlinecounselingpartners.com

3. Check out Laura's book: *Love Is an Action Verb* provides a deeper dive into the research, anecdotes, and examples of the concepts covered in this workbook. It is available from booksellers as a paperback, eBook and audiobook.

Acknowledgments

Writing a workbook about love would have been impossible without the boundless love and support I have received from the people in my world.

Thank you, Michael, for your unconditional love. You support every single day, believe in me and teach me how I can be a better partner.

JoJo and Nicky, you guys are extraordinary, and I'm honored and humbled to be your mom.

Mom, thanks for inspiring me to believe I can make a difference in the world.

Beta readers are unsung heroes in all publishing projects, but especially for a workbook! You guys took pen to paper, did the work, and volunteered your precious time to share your feedback. Thanks to you, this workbook has been tested in the real world.

Deep appreciation for Adam Hay, the talented internal book designer who brought this couples therapy workbook to life. You transformed my scribbles and visions into a beautiful and practical tool.

Jessica Kryzer and Hunter Beck, from Mindful Admins, thanks for being my "right-hand women." You guys are a remarkable marketing team, and I am especially grateful for your tireless positivity, hard work and passion.

Special thanks to cover designer Orlando Salazar, who built on the original work of Rodjie Ulanday, photographer Todd Zimmerman, and Susannah Worth for copy-editing.

Extraordinary gratitude to every single client who has been brave enough to enter my office, share your secrets, and teach me how to be a better therapist.

Thank you to the generous couples who volunteer to participate in research. We wouldn't know how to help people without you!

To John and Julie Gottman, and the entire Gottman Institute team, thank you for your mentorship, training, and research in creating a model that works.

I miss you, Dad, but you continue to inspire me every single day.

Appendix: Answer Keys for Practice Exercises

Chapter 3

Rule #1 Practice Worksheet

1. I feel **like** you need a new job.
2. I feel **that** the best way for us to be closer is for you to stop checking your email every five seconds.
3. I feel irritated when you look at your phone while we're talking.
4. I feel **like** I'm the only one working on this relationship.
5. I feel lonely when you have to work late.
6. I feel overwhelmed by everything that's on my plate right now.
7. I feel **like** you don't like spending time with me.
8. I feel **that** we only have sex when I initiate.
9. I feel shy about initiating sex.
10. I feel **like** I'm invisible.

Rule #2 Practice Worksheet

1. You have a great sense of humor. ~~when you're not being sarcastic.~~
2. Thanks for trying to help, ~~but you have no clue how to fold a load of laundry.~~
3. I'm sorry I raised my voice at you.
4. Thanks for helping me out with this email.
5. I'm sorry I'm late, ~~but there was an accident on the highway.~~
6. I'm so proud of you for going back to the gym.
7. You are a great listener, ~~when you're not texting.~~
8. I really appreciate that you surprised me at work for lunch, ~~but I'm still mad about the fight we had last night.~~

Rule #3 Practice Worksheet

1. I am worried about our finances.
2. I like my lasagna a little less well-done.
3. I am nervous that we won't make it to the show on time.
4. I missed you last night.
5. I disagree.
6. You are my best friend. (Trick questions, see rule exception)

Rule #4 Practice Worksheet

1. I've been feeling overwhelmed lately and would like to set up a time to re-visit how we divide household tasks.
2. I really like it when you talk to me about your feelings even though I know it's hard for you
3. I felt a little criticized when you said that.

Rule #5 Practice Worksheet

1. Always
2. Finally
3. Never
4. Always
5. Finally

Chapter 4

1. A. Let it slide
2. B. Talk it out
3. A. Let it slide
4. A. Let it slide
5. B. Talk it out

Chapter 5

Gentle Startup Practice Worksheet:

1. I feel frustrated and lonely when I am sitting alone waiting for you. Please call me by 5:30 and let me know your ETA.
2. I feel sad about how many of my mom's china plates have cracked. My request is for you to make sure none of the plates are touching each other in the dishwasher.

3. I feel criticized and like giving up when I work hard to do something you've asked me to do and am told I'm doing it wrong. I need you to try to notice what I am doing well in addition to giving me negative feedback.
4. I feel taken for granted when I hear how busy you are and how hard you work. Please try to remember we both work hard and are feeling overwhelmed right now.
5. I feel concerned about our budget. My request is for us to sit down together and talk about how to reach our savings goals.
6. I feel dismissed when you're on the phone while I'm talking. My request is for you to please put your phone down when we're talking about something important.
7. I feel rejected when you turn me down for lovemaking. My request is that we have a conversation about physical intimacy outside the bedroom to understand what we are both feeling.
8. I feel insecure about where I stand with you. I need to be reassured that you'd rather be with me than at work.

Chapter 6

Accountability Practice Worksheet

1. I definitely spent too much money on Christmas presents this year.
2. You're right, I was distracted, I'm sorry and am listening now.
3. I know I haven't been reaching out as much as I used to.
4. I don't want to scare you; I'll slow down.
5. I've been rescheduling our last few face-time calls, I'll try to find a better time that will work for both of us.
6. It sounds like you felt I was criticizing your parenting. Let me try saying it a different way.

Chapter 8

Skydiving Listening Practice Worksheet

1. A. Multitasking
2. B. Premature problem-solving
3. D. Playing devil's advocate
4. C. Not developing amnesia
5. B. Premature problem-solving
6. D. Playing devil's advocate

Validation Practice Worksheet

1, 4, 5, 7

Chapter 9

Intellectual Vulnerability Practice Worksheet

1, 3, 6, 8, 9

Emotional Vulnerability Practice Worksheet

1, 3, 5, 7, 9, 10

Physical Vulnerability Practice Worksheet

1, 3, 5, 7, 9. 10, 12

Notes

Forward
1. Origin unknown. Widely attributed to Lao Tzu, Chinese philosopher, 6th Century BCE.

Introduction
1. Gottman Institute. "The Gottman Method." The Gottman Institute, n.d., https://www.gottman.com/about/the-gottman-method/.
2. Sydney J. Harris ["Pieces of Eight" published in 1982. The quote appears on page 105] <- Adam I'll get the formatting right for this

Chapter 1
1. Henry David Thoreau, *Walden* (London: Pan Macmillan, 2016; originally published 1854).

Chapter 2
1. William Shakespeare, *The Merchant of Venice*, edited by Cedric Watts (Ware, England: Wordsworth Editions, 2000), 2.6:36.
2. John M. Gottman and Robert W. Levenson, "The Timing of Divorce: Predicting When a Couple Will Divorce Over a 14-Year Period," *Journal of Marriage and Family*, vol. 62, no. 3, 2000, https://doi.org/10.1111/j.1741-3737.2000.00737.x.
3. Widely attributed to Ralph Waldo Emerson, though may be derived from J. Elliot Cabot, "On the Relation of Art to Nature," *The Atlantic Monthly*, February 1864, https://www.unz.com/print/AtlanticMonthly-1864feb-00183.
4. Dalai Lama XIV (Tenzin Gyatso), *The Art of Happiness*, edited by Howard C. Cutler (Riverhead Books, 1998), p. 25.

Chapter 3
1. Barack Obama. (2016, July 12). Transcript: President Obama's remarks at Dallas memorial service. NPR. Retrieved from https://www.npr.org/2016/07/12/485605292/transcript-president-obamas-remarks-at-dallas-memorial-service

Chapter 4
1 Mary Parker Follett, Creative Experience (Eastford, CT: Martino Fine Books, 2013; originally published 1924), p. 300.
2 John Gottman, "The 5 Types of Couples," The Gottman Institute, 2014, https://www.gottman.com/blog/the-5-couple-types/.

Chapter 5
1. Oxford English Dictionary. "Criticism." Oxford University Press, 2021. 1. Widely attributed to poet and activist Maya Angelou (1951–2014).*Expert* (New York: Three Rivers Press, 1999), pp. 25–46.
2. John Gottman and Nan Silver, *The Seven Principles for Making Marriage Work: A Practical Guide from the Country's Foremost Relationship Expert* (New York: Three Rivers Press, 1999), pp. 25–46.

Chapter 6
1. Sometimes attributed to Aristotle, this quote likely originated with the writer, publisher, artist, and philosopher Elbert Hubbard (1856–1915), specifically his 1898 collection of short essays titled *Little Journeys to the Homes of American Statesmen*.
2 Gottman and Levenson, 2000.

Chapter 7
1. Widely attributed to Anne Lamott. However, it should be noted that there is no specific source or citation that can be attributed to this quote. It is possible that the quote is a paraphrase or summary of Lamott's various writings or speeches.
2. Lalah Delia, Vibrate Higher Daily: Live Your Power (Carlsbad, CA: Hay House, 2019).

Chapter 8
1. Brené Brown, *Daring Greatly: How the Courage to Be Vulnerable Transforms the Way We Live, Love, Parent, and Lead* (New York: Avery, 2015).

Chapter 9
1 Jon Kabat-Zinn, *Wherever You Go, There You Are: Mindfulness Meditation in Everyday Life* (New York: Hachette, 1994), p. 65.
2 Michel L. Dandeneau and Susan M. Johnson, "Facilitating Intimacy: Interventions and Effects," *Journal of Marital and Family Therapy*, vol. 20, no. 1, July 1994, https://onlinelibrary.wiley.com/doi/abs/10.1111/j.1752-0606.1994.tb01008.x.

Chapter 10
1 Amy Bloom, quoted in Julie Schwartz Gottman and John Gottman, *10 Principles for Doing Effective Couples Therapy* (New York: W.W. Norton & Company, 2015), p. 157.

Chapter 11
1. Arlen, H. & Harburg, E.Y. (1939). Over the Rainbow [Song]. In The Wizard of Oz [Motion Picture]. Metro-Goldwyn-Mayer.
2. Gottman and Gottman, 2015, p. 65.

Chapter 12
1. Tom Clancy quoted in David H. Freedman and Sarah Schafer, "Vonnegut and Clancy on Technology," inc.com, December 15, 1995.